Passive to Assertive

Speak Up, Set Boundaries, and Get What You Actually Want

A Workbook for Teens
Written by Andrew Hudson

© Copyright 2026 - All rights reserved.

The content contained within this book may not be reproduced, duplicated or transmitted without direct written permission from the author or the publisher. Under no circumstances will any blame or legal responsibility be held against the publisher, or author, for any damages, reparation, or monetary loss due to the information contained within this book, either directly or indirectly.

Legal Notice: This book is copyright protected. It is only for personal use. You cannot amend, distribute, sell, use, quote or paraphrase any part, or the content within this book, without the consent of the author or publisher.

Disclaimer Notice: Please note the information contained within this document is for educational and entertainment purposes only. All effort has been executed to present accurate, up to date, reliable, complete information. No warranties of any kind are declared or implied. Readers acknowledge that the author is not engaged in the rendering of legal, financial, medical or professional advice. The content within this book has been derived from various sources. Please consult a licensed professional before attempting any techniques outlined in this book. By reading this document, the reader agrees that under no circumstances is the author responsible for any losses, direct or indirect, that are incurred as a result of the use of the information contained within this document, including, but not limited to, errors, omissions, or inaccuracies.

Table of Contents

Introduction..5
   Communication Is Key..7
1. Life Won't Wait for You......................................15
   Why Henry Didn't Get the Job..............................17
   Life Is Cruel..22
   The Consequences of a Passive Lifestyle.............24
   The Cost of Bottled Emotions...............................33
   The Root Causes of Passivity................................40
   Building Self Awareness..45
2. Why Become Assertive?.....................................59
   The Assertive Image..61
   The Life You Want..67
3. Overcoming Obstacles to Assertiveness............74
   It's All in Your Mind...78
   Misconceptions About Assertiveness...................89
   Breaking Down Your Barriers...............................94
4. The Importance of Habits................................125
   Respect Yourself..129
   Speak Like You Mean It.......................................143
5. Assertiveness in Social Settings.......................156
   Understanding Social Interactions.....................158
   Practice Makes Perfect..175
6. The Key to Strong Relationships.....................189
   Understanding Relationships..............................193
   When Relationships Become Difficult...............218
7. Asserting Yourself in the Workplace...............228

Your Career and Reputation Matters............................ 230
Handling Adversity... 246
Conclusion...**261**
Test Yourself Everyday... 265
Key Points and Habits.. 268
References..**282**

Introduction

Mastering others is strength. Mastering yourself is true power. -Lao Tzu

If I'm going to make a strong case for why you should shift from being a passive observer in your own life to becoming the confident, assertive man you aim to be, I need to draw from real experience. While I won't focus too much on my own personal and professional journey, the lessons that truly resonate come from real-life examples, whether from family life, the workplace, sports, or business. Especially when viewed through the lens of leadership, these examples show what's possible when someone decides to take ownership of who they are and where they're going.

Even as you develop into an assertive man, you may never aspire to leadership. Instead, you may be quite happy to continue growing as a cooperative team player. But I could argue that leadership is not only inevitable but essential if you want to make progress in your life. And leadership, of course, starts with you. Let me start this guide to what is required of you as the leader of your soul. More specifically, let me provide you with a brief explanation of what is known as self-leadership.

Self-leadership is your ability to influence and direct your own personal thoughts and actions. These life-affirming thoughts and actions are what guide you to successfully achieve your goals and build the life you have always dreamed of leading.

Communication Is Key

But in order to lead a life that is satisfying, you will ideally be communicating with others for critical, non-judgmental perspectives and opinions. Rest assured that in this sense, the ability to communicate effectively with others will not break you, but will make you. As a leader of self, you will have more than enough confidence to make your own decisions and motivate yourself to take action in response to the decisions you have made, not just for yourself but for others, too.

Let me take this introduction a step further in asserting why communication remains key to your future success, whether as a footballer, a boxer, a trustworthy employee for a high performing company, a business leader, a devoted partner in a loving relationship or just a normal guy.

Arguably, one of the most important benefits of assertive communication is that you will be able to face confrontation head on and not shy away from it, in a way that respects the circumstances you find yourself in. Not only that, effective communication could be the deciding factor in helping you to secure your future dream job, or career, and maintain healthy relations with others. More importantly, how you communicate with yourself is key to your future success.

My Story So Far

In this guide, you will become familiar with Henry and Chris - two office workers looking to fill an available supervisor slot. As it stands, Henry is a reliable and trustworthy employee. His current supervisor knows that he can count on him to complete a majority of the tasks that form part of their department's core responsibilities. Chris, on the other hand, is an artful go-getter. He usually gets what he wants, and when he barks, others around him usually snap to attention. But most people in the office question whether Chris is also an honest, reliable, and trustworthy employee.

In the pages that follow, you will see who succeeds. By observing the habits, strategies and techniques provided throughout this book, you will decide for yourself whether it is worth keeping yourself rooted as a passive man like Henry.

Or, whether it is far better to be confident and always be able to trust your abilities, like Chris. Furthermore, I will share many experiences, both good and bad, of my transformation from passive to assertive.

Believe it or not, I was not always the confident, easy-going writer of self-help books, focusing mainly on the psychology of essential life-changing transformations for men.

The reason I am so passionate about publishing this guide is because I struggled with my identity and self esteem as a teenager and into my early adulthood, while I don't aim to make this a sob story about my life, I hope with this guide I can help boys and young men, like yourself, steer clear of the mistakes I once made, mistakes that brought unnecessary struggle and regret.

What This Guide Will Do For You

While my mistakes have shaped me into the man I am today, many of them turned into unhealthy habits that held me back from building healthy relationships, pursuing my dream career and enjoying my days as a young man.

Unfortunately I can't get those days back, but fortunately as a young man I eventually found something that always had my back.

Boxing.

Regular boxing training and being involved in a solid community helped set my head straight. I began prioritizing my health, I developed my social skills and I found purpose by setting myself a long term goal of competing in the ring. I did in fact reach that goal, but my competitive boxing career was very short lived - it wasn't for me. However I didn't stop there, many years of training later I became a qualified boxing coach and I still run my own sessions to this day. For the past few years I have taken great pride in teaching the techniques and principles of boxing to beginners, as for many youngsters, it is the beginning of a positive turning point in their life.

But my success only came through many months of trial-and-error perseverance while I learned to move my body and soul from being passive to assertive. And it wasn't until I qualified as a coach many years down the line that the others in the gym could finally take my guidance seriously, simply because I was able to assert myself.

I could only reminisce. What would life have been like for me if I had remained fixed in my passive shell?

This book will teach you about the art of being assertive in all areas of your life. Whether that be in school, sport, your personal life, or later on in your working life. As you read through this guide, you'll discover behaviors and habits that form the core of assertive communication. Habits are the foundation of lasting change, they shape our daily actions and, over time, influence who we become. In that sense, habits are the *'how'* - the engine that drives the shift from passive to assertive.

"Habits are the compound interest of self-improvement. The more you do them, the easier they become—and the stronger their impact grows over time." - James Clear

This guide will help you build the mindset you need to confidently navigate daily life and increase the chances that your needs are understood and met. It will help you to achieve your goals, whether to play for your local football team, to secure a second date with your crush, or to land a future job at a tech company that brings you a meaningful income. Your assertive nature will not put you at risk of losing control of your circumstances. Instead, it will help you to maintain control of your life.

Treat your assertive streak as a positive tool, living by the old adage that tools are only as good as their user. Remember that the ability to communicate assertively with others will strengthen your relationships and help you make a positive impact in social situations. More importantly, it will provide you with the motivational strength to pull yourself through tough times.

If it feels as though life is letting you down, remind yourself that you will always push through just as long as you are abiding by the rules of assertive communication techniques, as well as other life-transforming habits of health and self-awareness.

It is worth mentioning that throughout this guide, no matter your age, I will be referring to you as an assertive man. From this point on, you will take responsibility for your actions and begin your journey of personal growth, so if you are under the age of 18, don't think this guide doesn't apply to you.

Some boys become men not by age, but by circumstance.

Let's look into the lives of Chris and Henry. They are two sides of the same coin, facing in the opposite directions. While Chris has no issue with being the loudest in the room and he is used to gripping the hot-tempered bull by the horns. Henry, on the other hand, is as quiet as a whisper. Henry avoids confrontational situations as though they were the plague. Even though both Chris and Henry are vying for a promotion on offer, it would be dishonest of me to say that they are challenging each other. After all, as a rather passive man, Henry is offering little to no resistance to Chris's persuasive arguments for rewarding him with the position instead.

So, who gets the job in the end?

The Confidence Workbook

A hands-on guide containing 7 simple strategies designed to help you build self-esteem and develop confidence today.

Follow this link to get your **free** online copy

subscribepage.io/buildconfidence

1. Life Won't Wait for You

I was as gentle as a lamb led to the slaughter. I did not realize that they had plotted against me, saying, Let us destroy the tree and its fruit; let us cut him off from the land of the living, that his name be remembered no more.
–Jeremiah 11:19

In some ways, I could relate to what Henry was going through. For one thing, during my younger years I was just like Henry. But while I was able to break free from a train of passive habits that continued to set me back throughout my high school years and during my early years of meekly knocking on doors looking for a steady job, Henry's passiveness continued well into his professional life.

It should have come as no surprise to you to learn that, after a few days of deliberation and reporting back to management, George, the office manager, decided to appoint Chris as the new supervisor to the sales department, which was sorely in need of a facelift. Sales were down from one quarter into the next, and it was as clear as daylight that the company was under pressure to deliver a positive turnaround.

At the end of the day, it was the bottom line that counted, and finding the right man to respond to that line was a priority. George had concerns about Chris's abrasive manner of addressing his peers, sometimes even the customers, but nine times out of ten, Chris got the results that the company executives were looking for. While George still appreciated Henry's hard work and great results, George didn't see him fit for the additional responsibility, especially having to be the man who guides and motivates his team towards company goals.

Why Henry Didn't Get the Job

After giving Henry the news that his application had been turned down, it came as no surprise to George that Henry hardly batted an eyelid in response to the news. Offering no words of protest, Henry simply nodded his head, muttering under his breath, *"Fair enough."*

It was as if Henry was expecting the news that George was obliged to give. George had to wonder *"Why? Why bother at all? Why bother applying for a job you feel you have no chance of getting in the first place?"*

Anyhow, at least he applied. Perhaps this was a turning point in Henry's professional, and for that matter, personal life. Perhaps the next time an opportunity comes along for Henry, he will have learned lessons from this rejection.

So, why didn't Henry get the job?

Unlike Chris, Henry clearly wasn't a go-getter. He appeared to lack ambition, and his half-hearted response to the questions George raised during the interview was not impressive. The fact that he applied for a promotion did not hide the fact that Henry seemed to lack the drive required for a demanding and responsible position. He also clearly lacked the confidence and strong will to deal with a high-pressure environment. He showed poor leadership qualities, and thin-skinned, he appeared to be sensitive to other colleagues' reactions to his words and actions.

While Chris could bark an order with the snap of his fingers, hardly anyone could hear what Henry was saying, if he said anything at all. As I said in the introduction, communication is key, particularly in a role that requires responsibility, as well as supervisory, organizational, and leadership abilities. Effective communication in a leadership role requires the leader to not only communicate well verbally, but non-verbally too.

When we look back at some of the greatest leaders in history, many fit the image of wise, resilient men with a tough, composed presence, figures like Marcus Aurelius, Winston Churchill, and George Washington. While not all great leaders conform to this stereotype, and leadership today is increasingly diverse, with more women, younger individuals, and less traditionally stoic personalities rising to the top, there is one trait they all share:

The ability to communicate clearly, confidently, and effectively, especially under pressure.

When a leader remains composed under pressure, people naturally trust they have things under control, and often look up to them because of it. But leadership isn't just about guiding nations or commanding massive organizations. Realistically, most of us won't face that level of pressure. What's far more likely is that you'll have the chance to lead in everyday settings, whether it's a school club, your sports team, or a group project. And those moments matter.

So don't think that developing your leadership skills now is a waste of time. Your future employer will want someone who can stay calm and communicate clearly in a crisis. Your football team needs a voice when you're 1–0 down in the cup final with ten minutes to go. Every team, job, family, and community needs someone willing to step up and lead, and that someone can be you.

The Importance of Communication

Those whom the leader addresses take his every word seriously. They must know that he means every word he says, even if it's words they are not particularly thrilled to hear. Like being told to come in on icy-cold Saturday mornings to do a few hours of cold calling in order to achieve better sales returns by the next week. Whether it's desk clerks or factory floor workers, they are compelled to trust them, not just because of his words, but because his body language radiates composure, confidence, and a clear commitment to doing his best under the circumstances.

A good listener, a strong leader to boot, is also able to create for himself a better understanding of what those who follow him may be going through. He has a strong sense of what they may be feeling at any given time, and his ability to communicate effectively with others is healthy for the purpose of building better relationships with everyone. A good leader doesn't just bark orders expecting people to do all the dirty work on a Saturday to meet sales targets, he is turning up to work an hour before everybody else, reviewing the performance of his workers and offering assistance if required. Most importantly, he is making the phone calls himself: leading by example.

In the professional arena, he might be compelled to form good relationships with his workers, but at the same time, they get a sense that he wants to engage with them. They get a sense of his sincerity and interest in their well-being. They know, too, that they can rely on him to make effective decisions and resolve conflicts on their behalf. Moreover, they feel at ease discussing any personal challenges at home that might be impacting their well-being.

Whether at work, at school, in relationships, or in social settings, a good listener or leader doesn't necessarily have to assert himself, but he can be persuasive. He is able to communicate to others a persuasive argument that, ideally, they should follow his lead. At the same time, his confidence allows him to open his mind to alternative arguments.

Interestingly enough, good communicators who connect with others with empathy understand that the old adage that nice guys finish last might still be true.

Life Is Cruel

It might be true that nice guys finish last, but only if they let others and events in their lives get in their way. George knew this, but Henry didn't. And whether Chris knew or not would not have mattered. Chris was getting his way, and he couldn't have cared less what others may have thought of him. Or did he? It is interesting to note that, like passive men, aggressive men are also sensitive to what others may think of them. They use their shield of aggression to prevent others from hurting them.

But the common theme is that aggressive men, like Chris comes across as sometimes, get their way and passive men don't. It is rare for passive men to have their say. Indeed, as a grown man, Henry dreaded family get-togethers. To him, these days felt like endless occasions to justify why his dating life wasn't progressing the way that everybody expected, and each time he was asked about his career he struggled to convince anybody he was doing well for himself. Though his family's concern was well-meaning, Henry often felt under scrutiny, resenting the sympathy he received whenever he opened up about his struggles.

Life is cruel when you keep yourself rooted in passiveness. You are too afraid to speak out or speak up. Even if people chose to listen to you, they would more than likely argue right back in your face. Or so it felt for a passive young man like Henry. I know the feeling well.

After all, I was like Henry for many years.

The Consequences of a Passive Lifestyle

I know what it feels like to not get your way. I know what it feels like to not achieve your goals, even if they are modest in comparison to the achievements of others. I also know what it feels like to gaze at others: watching a man with his girlfriend in a coffee shop, watching another man slink into his souped-up convertible, and watching yet another man check the time on his Rolex wristwatch, adjusting his Cambridge-knotted tie, before briskly sweeping his way into the elevator to go to his top-floor office.

It is all in the imagination of a passive man who keeps to himself. On the surface, it might seem like others are successful. But if only he knew how to connect with others, he might know the truth of what really goes on in the minds of others. If they are successful in life, he is not jealous or envious of them, and he just wishes he could have what they seem to have. But little does he know; sometimes, in life, there is a high price to be paid for achieving success. Just because it appears a man is living a better life than you, doesn't necessarily mean it's true.

Sometimes, risks need to be taken. Come to think of it, isn't it true that the passive man is too afraid to take risks?

If you're still avoiding responsibility, like a wilting rose that does nothing to help itself, then it might not be the right time to take risks. First, you need to face the reality of your situation, own up to your role in it, and meet life's challenges with courage. Below are the many consequences that you'll face, or are currently facing, if you decide to stick to your passive ways:

- Low self-esteem and confidence. Feeling unworthy of healthy relationships, personal respect, or a successful career.
- Resentment and frustration. Believing it's unfair that other men achieve what you don't, breeding bitterness.
- Emotional dependencies. Relying on parents, partners, or friends to make decisions and validate your choices.
- Unhealthy habits and coping mechanisms. Suppressing emotions, isolating yourself, binge eating, compulsive gaming, or procrastinating.

- Poor mental and physical health. Struggling with anxiety, depression, chronic fatigue, or being overweight due to inaction and neglect.
- Lack of direction and purpose. Drifting through life with no clear goals, passion, or drive, leading to stagnation.
- Weak social and professional networks. Missing out on opportunities because of avoidance, fear of rejection, or poor communication skills.
- Financial instability. Failing to take initiative in your career or personal finances, leading to dependence or insecurity.
- Loss of respect from others. Friends, family, and colleagues may begin to see you as unreliable or incapable.
- Regret and wasted potential. Watching time pass as dreams fade, knowing deep down that you could have done more, been more.

Just one of these consequences is enough to leave you feeling low and worthless. But don't let thoughts of missed opportunities convince you that it's too late. You're still young, and that means time is on your side. The future isn't set in stone, and if you start now, it can only get better from here.

Passive Behaviors and Habits

"Oh look what the cats dragged in boys, Henry's showed his face!" It is the lunch break in the company's cafeteria the day after Chris was announced as the new supervisor. These are the bitter words of rebellious staff who've grown tired of how George has been keeping Henry in the job all these years. But they really don't have much to say anymore, they don't need to poke fun at him as it won't be long until new supervisor-elect, Chris arrives to bruise the poor man's emotions even further.

Even so, it is always challenging to taunt poor Henry. After all, he goes out of his way to avoid conflict. He sits in his corner in silence, munching on the peanut butter and jam sandwiches that his mother rustled up for him this morning. Yes, he still lives with his mother at his age! What a loser! He relies on her, and only on her, for comfort. He goes out of his way to please her. And yet still, he is doing so selfishly because he knows that he needs to keep this mother-son momentum going so that she can continue feeling sorry for him and pampering him like a wounded cat.

She tries to make decisions for him. If she doesn't, then who will? He isn't moving a muscle and can never seem to think for himself. It might be selfish as well, but there is one thing she is happy about: she can tell him to do anything. He will never say no to her. Even if her demands overwhelm him, and usually they do, he can't say no to her. Simply put, he has difficulty setting boundaries for himself.

The Image of a Passive Man

Henry's body language often revealed his nature long before he spoke, his supervisor and co-workers needed only to observe his facial expressions to sense his discomfort around them. Though he wasn't overtly difficult or disruptive, his reluctance to make eye contact during conversations left a negative impression. Alongside this, he displayed several other nonverbal cues that signaled passivity. To help you gain awareness of what passivity looks like, below shows a great list of common habits and behaviors that typically make a man appear passive:

Passive Body Language - Appearing Awkward

- Fidgeting, slouching, or making yourself appear smaller.
- Smiling nervously even when feeling uncomfortable.
- Lacking facial expressions.
- Having a closed off posture, tightly crossed arms.
- Avoiding eye contact.
- Touching face or neck frequently.

Passive Speech - Sounding Unconvincing

- Speaking with a soft tone at a low volume.
- Hesitant voice - speaking with an unsure tone, using a lot of filler words like *"Um," "I guess," "Maybe,"* and ending statements with upward inflection as if unsure.

Passive Interaction Behaviors

- Letting others interrupt you without protest.
- Nodding or agreeing with others excessively, even when you disagree.

- Standing or sitting on the edge of a group, or isolating yourself completely.
- Avoiding confrontation or conflict.
- Failing to express your personal needs, opinions or feelings, such as bottling up emotions and giving silent treatment when upset.
- Letting others make decisions for you.
- Apologizing excessively, even when not at fault.
- Avoiding responsibility or accountability, such as blaming others or not striving for progression with your career.
- Accepting blame for things that aren't your fault to avoid conflict.
- Avoiding setting boundaries with friends, family or co-workers.
- Not standing up for yourself in group settings.
- Giving in to peer pressure without objection.
- Being overly polite to the point of self-neglect.
- Holding back criticism or feedback to avoid upsetting others.
- Avoiding direct statements and instead hinting at things.

- Putting others' needs ahead of your own, even to your detriment.
- Over-explaining or justifying yourself when saying no.
- Feeling guilty for asserting yourself or asking for help.
- Feeling uncomfortable receiving compliments or downplaying achievements.
- Feeling unworthy of attention or recognition.
- Worrying excessively about what others think of you.
- Assuming your opinions or feelings don't matter.
- Avoiding difficult conversations instead of addressing issues.
- Feeling powerless to change your circumstances.

Even if you have made a habit of just one of the behaviors from the long list above, passivity fits you far better than assertiveness ever could. Also, considering you have purchased this guide, I assume you can relate to many of the above behaviors, especially in situations that make you feel uncomfortable - such as social settings, job interviews, around women or performance related activities.

We often do things that undermine us without even realizing it. A lack of self-awareness is one of the most common reasons why young men appear passive. Henry, for example, never intended to be disrespectful. However, because he felt more comfortable looking at the floor than making eye contact during conversations, and always isolated himself from group discussions, his co-workers perceived him as someone who isn't a team player.

No matter how hard Henry tried to do his best, there were still signs that he didn't care two hoots about the work he was supposed to be doing. But when he was compelled to respond to probing questions and taunts, he stammered and stuttered. It was always hard for his colleagues to make out what he was trying to say to them, so much so that after a while, most of them gave up talking to him at all.

It gave Henry a false sense of security. He could carry on with his day without any fear of being distracted. And yet still. Out of habit, he would continue to look over his stooped shoulders. Now that Chris had got the promotion, Henry would have to be on his guard even if it meant continuing to sink his head to the ground, trying to forget where he was.

Until the time came for Chris to take up his new role, he would continue to harass Henry at every chance he got. He was never impressed by Henry's poor social skills, especially since he had witnessed how confidently he could communicate with customers over the phone. Henry's sullen responses to Chris' taunts got him nowhere, either. George remained concerned about Henry's indecisiveness and continued to wonder how the poor man would cope once he was no longer under George's care.

The Cost of Bottled Emotions

The days are counting down until Chris starts his new role as supervisor and George fears that once the day comes, Henry would no longer be treated with kid gloves. In fact, the gloves might be removed altogether. George feared that Chris would resort to unorthodox and unlawful methods to get his way in the office. But this isn't the main worry.

While Henry offered no emotional response to his failure to secure a promotion, he let his poor mother have it in no uncertain terms. When she nagged him for whatever reason he should have been used to by now, he rebelled. He lashed out. He was argumentative. He was always making excuses, always blaming others for his poor state of affairs. He blamed his mother for his inability to find a decent girlfriend. He was misguided in his fear that all women were the same. Henry blamed his father for his inability to stand on his own two feet whenever he was challenged by his fears. Sometimes, he wished that his parents gave him more support, but then again, he never asked for it.

Are You Passive-Aggressive?

It is a misconception to suggest that you can eliminate your passive behavior through aggression. Instead of improving your relationships with others, you only make matters worse for yourself. Not only are your relationships damaged by your passive-aggressive defense mechanisms, it becomes even more challenging to repair your damaged reputation as well. You can check if you show signs of habitual passive-aggressive behavior by observing the following signs:

- You are bitter and resentful of the authority of those in positions of responsibility. For example, at work, you disagree with your manager's decisions but never express your concerns directly. Instead, you quietly resist by doing only the bare minimum, dragging your feet on tasks, or speaking poorly of him behind his back.
- You give the silent treatment to the people you care about, but when words come to mind, you are quick to blame them for your unhappiness. For example, after a disagreement with your friend, you stop speaking to

them for a full day. When they finally ask what's wrong, you say, *"You should already know"*.

- If you aren't somebody who always procrastinates, you delay a task in retaliation and it seems to others like you're choosing not to meet your responsibilities. For example, your friend, who recently annoyed you on a night out, asks you to help them move on Saturday. You agree but show up late, saying you were *"really tired"* or *"forgot the time"*. This happens often enough that others start to think you're intentionally unreliable or indifferent to their needs.
- You avoid direct communication but still expect others to understand and meet your needs. For instance, rather than telling your roommate you're upset about the mess in the kitchen, you make a sarcastic remark like, *"Must be nice not having to worry about cleaning up."*

While both aggression and passive-aggression stem from feelings of frustration, there's an important distinction between the two. Aggressive people tend to be direct, expressing their needs or emotions immediately, sometimes at the expense of others. Passive-aggressive people, on the other hand, often appear cooperative or agreeable on the surface, but express their negative feelings indirectly, through sarcasm, procrastination, backhanded compliments, or giving the silent treatment. They are two-faced if you like.

In many cases, passive-aggressive behavior develops when passive people, like Henry, allow resentment or discomfort to build up over time without addressing it. Eventually, those suppressed emotions leak out in subtle, unproductive ways, such as Henry giving his mother the silent treatment after having a stressful day at work. While being openly aggressive, like Chris can sometimes be, might get immediate results, it often damages relationships.

Still, at least the aggressive person communicates their needs.

That said, this isn't an invitation to become aggressive. The purpose of this guide is to help you become assertive: the ability to express your thoughts, feelings, and needs clearly and respectfully, without guilt, avoidance, or hostility.

A big reason many men decide to remain passive is because they mistake being assertive for being aggressive. While assertiveness does involve standing up for yourself, It's actually a healthy middle ground between passivity and aggressiveness. You don't need to raise your voice, insult others, or dominate conversations to be assertive. Unfortunately, this misunderstanding often keeps men stuck in passive habits. And as frustration builds, they lack a healthy outlet for their emotions. The result? Passive-aggressive behavior, which can also look like this:

- Backhanded compliments. *"You're surprisingly good at that, considering..."*
- Intentional ambiguity. *"Whatever you think is best."* (delivered with a dismissive or resentful tone)
- Intentional inefficiency. Doing a task poorly on purpose to show resistance or disagreement.
- Withholding information or support. Not passing along important information or refusing to help in subtle ways.
- Sabotaging plans subtly. *"Forgetting"* to make a reservation or bring something essential, then acting innocent.

- Feigning agreement. Saying *"Fine"* or *"It's okay"* while clearly being upset but refusing to talk about it.
- Using guilt-tripping language. *"I guess I'll just do it myself."*
- Giving dismissive or vague responses. Responding with *"Hmm"* or *"If you say so"* to shut down a conversation.

While that misconception is just one possible root cause of passivity, there are several others, often subtle, that quietly undermine your communication skills, strain your relationships, and create a range of other challenges. To truly move forward, you need to explore these influences deeper. Once you build self awareness and understand what's fueling your passive behavior, you can begin breaking these passive habits.

The Root Causes of Passivity

Perhaps it is a positive sign that you are not, by nature, an aggressive person. But you cannot deny that you still need to address your passive nature. By now, you have been provided with more than enough clues of the passive streak in a nice man who rarely gets his way and always seems to finish last. By now, after reading through the lists of passive and passive-aggressive behaviors, you've probably recognized a few patterns in yourself, and that's completely fine at this stage. We all fall into these habits from time to time. You might even recall moments when you stayed silent after being disrespected, or moments you didn't do something you wanted because you were worried about what others might think.

While these reflections may stir up feelings of regret or discomfort, try to hold onto them, they'll be useful for the three journaling exercises at the end of this chapter. These exercises are designed to help you process your experiences and begin shifting your mindset. Throughout this guide, you'll find many more exercises to take meaningful action.

These moments may have been missed opportunities in your life. While thinking about all those occasions where it seemed as though passivity, more than anything else, let you down, do not blame yourself. Do not blame others, either. You can still make things right. To understand your passive habits further, let's discuss the possible root causes of your passivity and where they stemmed from:

1. **Fear of rejection** - You might stay silent, avoid asking for help, or suppress your needs because you're afraid others will turn you down or distance themselves from you. This fear can make you prioritize acceptance over authenticity, often leading to people-pleasing or settling for less than you deserve.
2. **Fear of conflict** - You may avoid expressing disagreement or setting boundaries because you dread the idea of arguments or tension. This fear stems from the belief that conflict will lead to rejection, punishment, or emotional harm. As a result, you give in or stay quiet, even when something bothers you deeply.

3. **Fear of judgment** - You might avoid speaking up out of worry that others will think you're wrong, dramatic, or incapable. This fear can keep you stuck in self-censorship, second-guessing your thoughts and ideas instead of expressing them confidently.
4. **Fear of failure** - You might hold back from pursuing goals or trying new things because you're afraid of making mistakes or letting others down. This fear traps you in hesitation, causing you to play it safe instead of taking the risks needed for growth.
5. **Poor self-esteem** - When you don't believe in your own worth, it's hard to think your needs or opinions matter. You may shrink yourself in social settings, doubt your abilities, and let others take the lead, even when you feel otherwise.
6. **Your environment** - Whether at home, work, or school: toxic environments can condition you to stay quiet or compliant. If your surroundings don't feel emotionally safe, passivity becomes a form of self-protection.
7. **Seeking validation** - If your sense of worth depends on how others perceive you, you may prioritize pleasing others above standing up for yourself. You

might avoid saying *"no"* or expressing disagreement out of fear it will cost you approval or affection.

8. **Past experiences** - Bullying, emotional neglect, or abuse can deeply damage your sense of safety and agency. Trauma can train your nervous system to expect danger in confrontation, pushing you toward withdrawal, appeasement, or silence to survive.

9. **Personality** - If you're naturally introverted or highly sensitive, you may be more reflective, quiet, or conflict-averse by default. That doesn't mean you're doomed to be passive forever, but it might take extra intentionality to develop assertiveness that feels authentic to you.

10. **Poor upbringing** - If your upbringing lacked emotional support, communication skills, or strong adult guidance, you may have missed essential tools for healthy self-expression. Furthermore if you lacked positive role models or were taught that showing emotions are a sign of weakness, you may struggle to be open about your needs. Without clear guidance, it's hard to know who you're meant to become, but fortunately, this guide is here to change that.

After watching Chris finally step into the supervisor role, the position Henry had quietly hoped would be his, he's hit a turning point. Still stuck in the same role he's held for years, Henry feels a deep yearning for change. He's had enough.

But the question remains: where does he start?

Building Self Awareness

Before you can stand up for yourself, you have to know what you're standing for. That's where self-awareness comes in. Asserting yourself starts with understanding your own feelings and needs. Self-awareness helps you recognize when something doesn't sit right, when you're being overlooked, or when you're just going along with things to avoid conflict. It gives you the clarity and confidence to speak up and make yourself heard in a way that's true to who you are.

When it comes to addressing passive behavior and replacing it with assertiveness that empowers people to face life's challenges, Albert Ellis's Rational Emotive Behavior Therapy (REBT) stands out as a powerful approach. You see, REBT is quite the opposite of passive talk therapy. While passive talk therapy is where the therapist mostly listens without offering much guidance, challenge, or active intervention, REBT is a structured, action-oriented form of therapy that helps individuals identify and challenge irrational beliefs.

We could argue that an excessive amount of aggression expressed in the workplace, at home, or even on the football pitch is indeed unhealthy and can be addressed through REBT. But what about passivity? Is it irrational? Or is it a fair way to solve problems or make things right during a crisis?

The first and most reliable sign that you're gaining control over your life is developing the habit of regularly understanding your thoughts, emotions, and behaviors. With this awareness, it's only a matter of time before you fully take charge. In fact, the best approach is to start acting as if you are already an assertive man, modeling your behavior and mindset around that belief.

As intrigued as I remain about Albert Ellis's pioneering theories on REBT, let us use this therapy as a self-help model to enhance our own levels of self-awareness. Doing so will also allow you to identify, challenge, and replace self-defeating beliefs with healthier ones that promote emotional well-being and goal achievement. While it no doubt took a lot longer to develop than it did learning our ABCs at nursery, Ellis's version of his psychology-based ABCs also highlights the following:

- **Activating event** - Look for the events or circumstances that trigger your negative emotional responses. Also question whether you've built unhealthy habits because of certain events.
- **Belief** - Examine what you believe about the event, and more importantly, about yourself because of it.
- **Consequence** - Look at the emotional and behavioral results of that belief.

This simple exercise, which is soon to be covered in great detail, is designed to help you explore the experiences and situations that may have shaped your passive behavior. By reflecting on these patterns, you'll gain a deeper understanding of your passive habits and what keeps them going. With that awareness, you can begin to create a practical plan to replace passive behaviors with assertive ones.

Exercise 1 - Identify Your Passive Behaviors

It's important to note that some of these exercises may stir up intense emotions, especially as you begin to explore past experiences, limiting beliefs, and deeply rooted patterns of behavior. This is a normal part of the growth process, but it can feel overwhelming at times. If you find yourself struggling, consider doing the exercises with someone you trust, such as a close friend or mentor. Alternatively, take regular breaks and give yourself space to process what comes up.

So, this first exercise is about building your self awareness to a very basic level, so it is crucial that you are able to identify all of your passive behaviors and the events that trigger them.

Very simple: revisit the list of passive behaviors from the section *"The Image of a Passive Man"* and write down the ones that resonate with you. If you're having trouble recalling these moments, try reflecting on times when you felt uncomfortable, such as first dates, job interviews, sporting competitions and large group settings. Passive behavior often shows up in moments of discomfort, in these situations you might have held back, stayed silent, or avoided action.

Think about what you were doing/avoiding in those moments?

Following that, start looking for repeated patterns in the situations that trigger your passive responses. For example, you might realize that whenever you're asked to speak up in a classroom full of people, you feel anxious about being the center of attention and it causes you to hesitate, even though you'd have no trouble expressing your thoughts clearly in a more private setting. As you link your past life experiences and passive behaviors, you can see how they turn into passive habits, therefore causing you to be a passive person. Below is an example of this exercise, remember it doesn't have to be perfect.

- **Passive behavior:** Crossing my arms tightly - I do this a lot when speaking to people I'm not comfortable around as I'm not sure whether they like me or not.
- **Passive behavior:** Avoiding conflict - I find it uncomfortable to disagree with my dad as I think he

may tell me off, so I agree with him even when I don't like what he has to say.
- **Passive behavior:** Avoiding eye contact - When I meet someone new, I often break eye contact quickly because I worry they might think I'm strange.

At this stage, keep things simple. The purpose of this exercise is to help you become more aware of how passivity shows up in your life, even in ways you might not have recognized before. You may not have realized that your reactions in certain situations were passive, but increasing your awareness is the first step toward change.

Exercise 2 - Identify Your Passive-Aggressive Behaviors

You may argue that there is not an aggressive bone in your body, but the purpose of this exercise is to reflect on moments when you felt frustrated about not getting your needs met, and instead of expressing it directly, you responded in a subtle or indirect way. And no, we're not talking about throwing a tantrum at your sixth birthday party over not getting the toy you wanted. Grab a pen and paper, and think back to real situations that caused you to react in one of the following passive-aggressive ways. Jot them down, along with any consequences that followed.

- Denying when upset about something, but your actions say otherwise.
- Deliberately under-communicating.
- Silent treatment.
- Complaining behind somebody's back instead of addressing the issue.
- Playing the victim.
- Subtle digs.
- Intentionally forgetting things or doing things poorly.

This reflection is a powerful step toward greater self-awareness and change, but only if you keep this list and refer to it each time that your life doesn't go the way you want. The truth is, setbacks, rejection, and frustration are inevitable. And in those moments, it's easy to slip back into old, passive-aggressive habits that quietly sabotage your relationships and your growth. Let this list serve as a reminder: reacting indirectly only creates more issues. Yet again, below is a short example of how to complete this exercise in case you are stuck.

- When I was rejected by my crush to go out for a date, I made many snide comments about her to my friends - this led to my crush losing all respect for me and it also damaged my reputation.
- When I received constructive criticism from my football coach about my performance at half time, I responded with phrases like *"It's not just me playing bad"* or *"You don't speak to the rest of the team like this"* - this led to the coach taking me off for the second half and having a word with me to work on my attitude.

Exercise 3 - Building Self-Awareness with REBT

For the final reflective exercise of this chapter, we'll revisit the REBT ABC method introduced in the *"Building Self-Awareness"* section. This time, however, we'll go beyond analyzing isolated events and take a deeper look at the internal beliefs that have shaped your passive habits over time. While Exercise 1 focused on specific situations that triggered passive behaviors, this activity challenges you to examine your ongoing inner dialogue. Usually it is the case that each time life doesn't go your way, your negative beliefs are often reinforced, strengthening the passive habits you've developed. Therefore use the REBT ABC method to identify and understand your inner beliefs so you can work on changing them, below is an example.

- **Activating event** - Regularly being interrupted or spoken over in group discussions at work.
- **Belief** - I feel worthless, as if my opinions don't matter to anybody.
- **Consequence** - I feel safer isolating myself from groups because being interrupted makes me feel small and helpless. This is a passive habit of mine and this regular isolation causes me to have nobody to express

my emotions to at work, this is a big reason why I don't like my job.

Questions for Disrupting Irrational Beliefs

- *Is this belief based on facts or assumptions?* This belief is just an assumption. While being frequently interrupted feels frustrating, it doesn't actually prove that I am worthless.
- *Is there evidence for this belief?* While I have been interrupted multiple times by the same people, the only evidence is me telling myself that I'm worthless, which isn't valid.
- *Is there evidence against this belief?* Yes. They could be interrupting because of excitement, poor listening skills, cultural habits, not realizing they're doing it or because they are bullies. Plus, people outside of work listen to me respectfully.
- *What's a more rational belief I can adopt?* I only feel like I don't matter in my head, but that doesn't mean it's true. People have shown they care about me before and on many occasions I have positively contributed to a group discussion. Instead I can begin to believe

that I am an important member of any group discussion.
- *What action can I take to adopt this rational belief?* I can begin by staying present and contributing more in group discussions at work, even if I am interrupted. I can take it further by finding group discussions outside of work in subjects I'm passionate about, such as sports, to prove to myself that I am valued in a group setting.

Whether or not you personally relate to the example, the REBT ABC journaling method is a powerful tool you can use to challenge any negative beliefs that may be holding you back. I encourage you to make a habit of using this method, not necessarily every day, but especially when you begin to notice recurring thought patterns that undermine your self-worth. That's your signal to pause, reflect, and reframe those beliefs through awareness and journaling.

Remember, you're just getting started. Writing thoughts and feelings down will help you build awareness, but true change happens when you take action. To truly shift your mindset, you'll need to go out into the world and gather real-life evidence that supports your new, more rational beliefs. Which is why the last step of REBT ABC remains important.

Now it's your turn, grab a pen and paper and note down your life experiences which have caused you to build passive habits using the REBT ABC method. For step A, think about what day to day events make you feel anxious, helpless or frustrated? For step B, think about what irrational belief is behind your passive behavior. For step C, think about the consequences of your passive behavior. Finally, ask yourself the following questions to reframe your irrational beliefs:

- *Is this belief based on facts or assumptions?*
- *Is there evidence for this belief?*
- *Is there evidence against this belief?*
- *What's a more rational belief I can adopt?*
- *What action can I take to adopt this rational belief?*

As this chapter comes to a close, it's worth mentioning a few things. First and foremost, focus only on what you can control. In the earlier example, he couldn't control whether others interrupted him in a group discussion, but he could control how he responded. Instead of storming off in frustration, he chose to remain present. Over time, as he stopped reacting emotionally to deliberate interruptions, those seeking a reaction lost interest.

As you move from passivity toward assertiveness, you'll face daily challenges that push you out of your comfort zone. The key is to regularly practice self-awareness so you can take thoughtful, deliberate action to build assertive habits, across all kinds of situations. Which is why pairing journalling with actionable tasks is important.

It won't always be easy. You will make mistakes. You may feel embarrassed. But remember, every setback is an opportunity to grow, not a verdict on your worth or ability. Everyone experiences challenges. A single failure doesn't define you. If something goes wrong, reflect on it. Ask yourself what you could have done differently, and plan how you'll handle it next time. Don't see mistakes as proof you're not good enough, see them as feedback for your progress.

In addition to journaling, consider seeking feedback from people you trust. This isn't a sign of weakness, it's a sign of courage and self-respect. Trusted friends or mentors can help you uncover strengths and blind spots you might not see yourself.

Also, be mindful not to dwell on your negative thoughts and emotions for too long. While it's important to acknowledge and understand them, ruminating can reinforce your pain rather than resolve it. That's why these exercises ask you to write down past negative experiences, not to live in them, but to gain clarity about how they've shaped passive habits and to recognize the consequences they bring. Once they're on paper, you can choose to let go, or revisit them only as reminders of why staying passive doesn't serve you.

Finally, attempt to shine light on your negative experiences. For example, if the reason why you have developed passive habits was because you were bullied earlier in life, don't just remember the shame or isolation, remember that you survived it. You endured something painful and kept going. That strength is real. And it proves that you're capable of facing whatever challenges lie ahead.

I hope that was motivating enough for you...

2. Why Become Assertive?

Being assertive does not mean attacking or ignoring others feelings. It means that you are willing to hold up for yourself fairly without attacking others. – Albert Ellis

As a boxing coach, I was more than familiar with the Chinese legend Lao Tzu. It was through following the career of kung fu icon Bruce Lee that I came across Tzu's inspirational quotes. I read the Bible occasionally, but I am not religious. Like other spiritual texts, you sometimes stumble across interesting, thought-provoking passages. They make you think about your life so far.

They can also motivate you to change your ways of behaving, in this case, learning to assert yourself in your personal life. Past experience has also shown me that calculated physical and verbal assertiveness also has its place in sports. I think back to the way legendary Manchester United team captain Bryan Robson was able to compose himself whenever he was under pressure. I think back to boxers like Sugar Ray Leonard, who always appeared to be up against far more powerful forces in the ring.

But not players like Eric Cantona, who, at one stage, seemed to confuse kung fu with football when reacting to a bout of verbal abuse from a disgruntled spectator. Not even the great Muhammad Ali, who sometimes seemed to spend more time fighting with his mouth than with his fists. And certainly not Mike Tyson, who physically humiliated Larry Holmes back in the day.

But who is Albert Ellis? I wondered.

Ellis was not a warmonger, nor a fighter. He was not a boxer either, and no, there was no indication that he was ever interested in the game of gridiron football, seeing that he hailed from the USA. More importantly, Albert Ellis was a psychologist who founded what is known as rational emotive behavior (REBT) - the exercise we covered in the previous chapter! Not reading too much into what Ellis did, it does sound like he created a positive response to the unhesitant, uncertain behavior of people who lacked enough assertiveness to tackle some of life's toughest decisions.

Like deciding when was the right time to strike back as a form of defense against a marauding army that was about to destroy and raze a town to the ground.

The Assertive Image

A month has passed since stepping into his new role as supervisor and Chris was almost unrecognizable. It wasn't the slicked-back hair that caught everyone's attention, it was the unexpected shift in his demeanor. To the surprise of his colleagues, the outbursts of aggression that once defined his presence had almost ceased to exist. What's surprising is that Chris never went to see a therapist to seek help for his aggressive behaviors, it was as though he woke up one day and decided that it was time for him to change. As a workplace supervisor, he was now the adult in the room, never mind that his peers were, more or less, the same age as he was.

Thankfully for Chris and those he now leads, his natural inclination to be assertive when it counts has never left him. It is a way to get things done without hurting or offending others. For Chris, it is an excellent means of communicating his needs to others. While not seeking therapy, he started keeping a very basic journal, similar to exercise 2 listed in this guide, making an effort to look back on times where he offended others by raising his voice or rudely demanding things. He can now see how his previously thoughtless behavior could have had something to do with a lack of education and influence, just as is the case with passive behavior.

He surprised himself sometimes, seeing how assertive, rather than aggressive behavior, let him clearly express his needs, get results from his workers, and do so without causing hurt or offense. Furthermore, he has received plenty of praise from others with his new approach to handling tasks in the office.

Assertive Behaviors

Chris' mature approach to his newly created work-life balance allowed him more clarity in his thoughts, which he seemed to have no difficulty in sharing with others. I think this may have had more to do with his increased levels of confidence. We now know that he was cool in the company of others, but it was his self-assurance, without needing to be aggressive, that sealed the deal where it counted.

Chris had no problem with retaining his use of "I" statements. He was quite used to this practice by now. But now, owning his feelings came with a difference. Today, Chris seems to have a more acute understanding of what others may go through when they are under severe pressure. He no longer blames them when things aren't going right. He tries his best not to lash out at Henry either.

So, Chris is doing well for himself, unfortunately we can't say the same for Henry right now, but at least he is inspired by Chris' new attitude in the office. While we've already reviewed the small but significant changes he's made in his behaviors and habits, below is an extensive list of assertive behaviors and examples that serve as valuable examples to aspire to.

- Clear and direct communication. Expressing your thoughts and feelings openly without beating around the bush. *"I won't be able to meet the deadline for the report by Friday. I need another 3 days to complete it thoroughly."*
- Using *"I"* statements. Taking ownership of your feelings. *"I feel frustrated when meetings start late, I have things to do please can we start them earlier"*

- Maintaining appropriate eye contact. Keep it balanced, natural and steady, about 50–70% of the time in conversation, enough to show interest, not so much it feels intense.
- Calm and steady tone of voice. Speaking firmly but respectfully, avoiding yelling or being overly soft.
- Setting and respecting personal boundaries. Saying *"No, I don't want to go for drinks after work,"* without expressing guilt or over-explaining.
- Active listening. Paying full attention when others speak and acknowledging their views. Leaning into the conversation to show interest, asking clarifying questions and acknowledging their feelings.
- Expressing disagreement respectfully. Saying *"I see your point, but I think this is a better way of completing the task"* instead of avoiding conflict or attacking.
- Accepting constructive criticism gracefully. Listening without becoming defensive or dismissive.
- Asking for help when needed. Requesting assistance clearly and without apology for your needs, there's no shame in asking for help, we all need help!

- Standing up for yourself without aggression. Defending your rights or opinions calmly when challenged.
- Confident body language. Standing or sitting up straight with your shoulders relaxed but not slouched. Using purposeful gestures, like hand movements that match your words. Take up plenty of space, don't hide yourself from anybody.
- Taking responsibility for your actions. Owning up straight away when you make a mistake at work.
- Expressing appreciation and giving compliments. Communicating positive feelings genuinely and appropriately. People like being complimented.
- Being comfortable with silence. Allowing pauses in conversation without rushing to fill them (don't confuse this with hesitation).
- Negotiating and compromising when appropriate. Finding mutually beneficial solutions without giving up your core needs. Meeting in the middle.

Now, you certainly don't have to religiously do all of the above at all times to be considered assertive, what matters most is developing the habit of communicating in a way that confidently expresses your needs, while still being respectful of others.

Throughout this guide you will find many examples of assertive communication, please do not make a rash decision to copy all of the phrases and add them into your daily vocabulary, doing so will ruin your authenticity. Becoming assertive isn't a copy-and-paste method. True assertiveness comes from expressing your needs, which are personal to you. It requires you to face your fears, challenge negative beliefs, and take action to break unhealthy habits.

To truly grow, you need to overcome your own specific obstacles. That's exactly what we'll explore in the next chapter. This journey takes time, and it won't be easy, but it will be worth it. The best way to overcome your personal challenges is through regular self reflection and consistent practice. While we'll dive deeper into common obstacles, such as fear, poor self esteem, and misconceptions, it's important first to explore something even more foundational: your motivation. Because no lasting change happens without a clear sense of why. Understanding your reason for wanting to become more assertive is the fuel that will keep you moving forward, especially when it gets tough.

The Life You Want

Let's be real, as men, we all secretly want to be like James Bond. He's effortlessly cool, sharp-witted, impeccably dressed, and always seems to always know exactly what to do and what to say. Calm, composed, and confident under pressure, Bond exudes a level of assertiveness that most people admire. Of course, he's not the perfect role model as he tends to hide his emotions behind a tough exterior. But hey, nobody's perfect.

Henry and James Bond actually have a few things in common: they both appreciate beautiful women, enjoy a good drink, have a taste for flashy cars, and value stylish accessories. The key difference? Bond actually gets those luxuries, cruising in Aston Martins and charming his way through glamorous encounters. Henry, on the other hand, hasn't been on a date in years and drinks most nights after work to cope with a life that doesn't feel fulfilling.

But here's the thing, Henry has something that even Bond doesn't talk much about: a clear why. The more he journaled, which he's started to build a great habit of weeks following the failed promotion, the more he realized that expressing his needs in a healthy, assertive way could actually get him what he wants. Which for Henry was to begin dating, earn a promotion, and stop getting disrespected at work.

Despite his frustrations, Henry is motivated to change and is actively working on it.

Sure, he still tends to be overly critical of himself. But he's now asking the right questions: *What must I do to change? What's holding me back?* And you're doing the same, spending more time processing your internal world. That matters. Just remember: don't be too hard on yourself. Change is happening, even if it's not always obvious.

Here's the bottom line: positive change should lead to a better life. There's no point in doing the hard inner work if it doesn't lead somewhere meaningful. And let's be honest, we all want a better life. More fulfilling relationships, financial growth, new experiences, and a sense of confidence that feels real. That kind of life? It starts with becoming more assertive. See below for some of the many benefits it can bring.

- **Stronger self-confidence** - By speaking up for yourself reinforces the belief that your thoughts, feelings, and needs are valid. Therefore, you feel more secure in who you are and what you stand for.
- **Healthier relationships** - Assertiveness creates mutual respect and honesty in friendships, family dynamics, and dating. You attract people who value and respect your boundaries.
- **Less stress and anxiety** - When you suppress your needs, resentment builds. Assertiveness releases that pressure. You feel calmer, more in control, and less overwhelmed.
- **Improved communication skills** - You learn to express your needs clearly, listen actively, and people begin to enjoy speaking to you. Conversations become more honest, productive, and drama-free. Knowing how to say *"no"* protects your time, energy, and emotional safety.
- **Increased respect from others** - People respect those who respect themselves. You're seen as someone with confidence, integrity, and leadership potential.
- **Greater independence** - Assertiveness helps you speak up about what you want in life, whether it's

career goals, friendships, or values. You take control of your future instead of letting others steer it.

- **Conflict becomes easier to handle** - Assertiveness equips you with tools to address issues without blowing up or shutting down. You face problems directly and solve them without damaging relationships.
- **Authentic self-expression** - You stop hiding parts of yourself to fit in. You live with more honesty and alignment with your values and beliefs.

Exercise 4 - Your Call to Assertiveness

Leading on from the previous motivational spell, simply spend 5 minutes writing down all the reasons why you want to become assertive. Be honest and specific. Maybe it's to sound more convincing in conversations, to feel more confident on the sports field, to ask for what you deserve at work, or to stop second-guessing yourself in social situations. Whatever your reasons are, they matter.

Once you've written them down, don't just tuck the list away and forget about it. Keep it somewhere visible and easily accessible, a notebook you carry with you, your phone, your bathroom mirror, or even your desk. This list is your why. It's the reminder of what's at stake and what's possible.

On the days when progress feels slow, or you slip back into old habits, look at that list. Let it ground you. Let it remind you of the life you're working toward—the confidence, the respect, the inner calm.

Exercise 5 - Little But Often

I'll admit, the long list of assertive behaviors covered earlier in this guide is a lot to take in, you may think that is plenty of change for you to make, especially in a short space of time, so with this exercise you will be taking action with just one behavior and building a habit of it. In fact, real growth starts with small, consistent action.

Choose just one behavior from the list of assertive behaviors earlier on in this guide, and begin building a habit of it. Focus on applying it in your daily communication for the next week. Keep it simple and manageable, you're not trying to transform overnight, you're creating a solid foundation.

A great place to start is learning to say *"no"* to things you don't want to do, without over-explaining yourself or feeling guilty. This is one of the most powerful signs of assertiveness. When someone asks something of you that doesn't align with your priorities, it's perfectly okay to say, "*No, I'm not able to,*" or simply, "*No, I'd rather not.*" You don't owe people elaborate justifications, and you certainly don't need to apologize for honoring your boundaries.

That said, use your judgment. If your teacher asks you to complete an assignment, or your parents ask for help around the house, those are responsibilities, not boundary violations. This exercise isn't about avoiding what's required of you; it's about practicing assertiveness in situations where you tend to put others first at the expense of your own well-being. For example, turning down a friend's request to help with homework when you're already overwhelmed with your own is a great starting point.

To end this chapter, remember that what others might be thinking of you during this transformational stage remains unimportant, while this at first is difficult to keep in mind, the more time you spend doing things you want to do the less you begin to care about other's opinions as life goes on. Focus on how these changes make you feel. The longer you practice assertive behaviors the sooner you will notice the difference it makes to you as a man. And the sooner others will notice, too. Always remember that practice makes perfect.

3. Overcoming Obstacles to Assertiveness

Obstacles don't have to stop you. If you run into a wall, don't turn around and give up. Figure out how to climb it, go through it, or work around it - Michael Jordan

It's now been two months since Chris stepped into his role as supervisor. He continues to perform well, no longer throwing his weight around in the rude manner he once did. Though he's certainly far from perfect, there are still moments when he loses his temper. However, his growing self-awareness allows him to quickly recognize when he's slipping into old aggressive habits, and he is able to use effective coping strategies to get back to assertive ways.

I bet you're wondering, how's Henry getting along?

The past couple of months have been challenging for Henry. He has made significant changes, including practicing regular self-reflection with journalling, joining the local gym and committing to four tough workouts a week, improving his eating habits, and immersing himself in self-help books.

While he hasn't particularly enjoyed this sudden change to his lifestyle, he knew what he did each day would help him in the long run. Especially with his consistent reflection as he's begun to understand himself more deeply. For instance, the root causes of his passiveness, what situations make him uncomfortable, what he fears each day, which passive behaviors he has made a habit of and why he wants to become assertive.

He's started peeling back the layers. But he knows the journey isn't over. Self awareness is one thing, but putting that insight into action by practicing assertiveness is the real challenge ahead.

He's pleased with the progress he has made with his appearance and pleasantly surprised by his own discipline in maintaining these habits, but he still finds himself stuck at a crossroad. He wants to speak up and say what's on his mind, but something always holds him back. He worries about saying the wrong thing, offending someone, or being seen as rude. So instead, he stays silent or resorts to saying what's expected, even when he feels frustrated, dismissed, or uncomfortable.

This even stays true at home, he avoids conflict with his mother by simply nodding along. Deep down, Henry is tired of feeling invisible. But becoming assertive isn't just about talking louder; it's about facing the fears and negative beliefs that have kept him silent for so long.

The barrier between self-reflection and action is often fear. For Henry, that fear runs deep. He's written out countless tasks to work on becoming assertive, yet he hesitates to follow through, worried he'll mess things up. On many occasions, he's crossed out tasks and rewritten them, trying to perfect an action he hasn't even taken. He's stuck in his head, overthinking to the point that the longer he delays, the harder it becomes to move forward. It's not just failure he fears — it's rejection, conflict, and judgment. Still, Henry has learned that failure isn't the end of the world. After all, he's already faced it.

It never occurred to him that, unlike them, at least he applied for the promotion.

What was it that Henry read about the great war-time leaders during his hours of isolation behind closed doors in his bedroom, with only his library books for company? While

Roosevelt remarked that the only thing to fear was the very thought of fear, Churchill cajoled those who would listen that they should never, ever give up on what they are attempting.

Attempting the impossible, perhaps?

He wanted to firmly stand up to the bullies at work who had long manipulated him into taking on their extra tasks. He wanted to speak with confidence and be taken seriously. Having already proved to himself that he could stick to new habits, he decided it was the right time to start confronting his fears, he started by asking himself...

What am I really afraid of? What's the worst that could happen? Where do these fears come from? And what small steps can I take to start facing them?

It's All in Your Mind

Change begins in the mind. Before any goal is achieved or habit is built, the mind must first believe it's possible. Your mindset shapes how you see the world, how you respond to challenges, and whether you push forward or give up. It can be your greatest obstacle or your most powerful tool, and you are the only person who can determine which it will be.

My father often reminded me that I am the only one responsible for my actions — that no one else can control how I choose to respond or behave. He said that no matter what I had failed at during my early adult life; I hadn't let anyone down but myself. If anyone had to be disappointed, it had to be me. He also instilled in me the belief that no matter how much others could or would help me out of my passiveness, only I could help myself if I wanted to see positive results.

I am happy to say that as far as Henry is concerned, the seed of will was planted the day his promotion application was turned down. I know that you want to make changes as well. You wouldn't be reading Passive to Assertive otherwise, would you? Where there is a will, there is a way.

Mindset Theories

Begin by saying to yourself that no matter what or who you are faced with, you can overcome it. It is just a matter of finding workable solutions. I learned to appreciate this growth-oriented mindset from the days when I was faced with formidable opponents in the boxing ring. After I hung up my gloves for good, I could instill what I like to call the David vs. Goliath mentality in the students I was mentoring.

They might not have been able to floor an opponent twice their size. They didn't need to run a mile from him, either. What they could do is deck their opponents with the element of surprise, figuratively speaking, of course. Because of your reputation for being docile, your perceived enemies won't know what hit them. Long before you deliver the killer punch, they must not know what you are planning. You could create this element of surprise by acting assertively in a social setting, when normally you would sit in the corner hoping that everybody would leave you alone, you could approach the group of people having a conversation and chime in your opinion loudly and clearly. This simple change to your behavior, which may at first shock the others, allows you to put the foot in the door to become known as assertive. Repeating actions like these eventually move you from the corner to the room, to the center of attention, depending if that's what you're after.

But you must know what you intend to do to deal with a confrontational situation. You can do that by developing what is known as the growth mindset. What is interesting to note about the growth mindset is that it is not a once-off learning curve. It is a lifelong learning experience that teaches you to appreciate that this is all it takes: Your most basic abilities, whether communicating with others or addressing your most primitive fears, can be developed through dedication and hard work. Therefore, this is a habit for you to build.

Before we get into the growth mindset, I'd like to share a big mistake of mine. I had this self belief ingrained in me that I could only begin to act assertively once I have achieved my goals, which at the time was to be in good shape and earn a fair bit more money than the average wage. This mindset seriously limited my progress as I was waiting for something to happen that had absolutely nothing to do with developing my communication skills. While getting in shape and increasing my income helped boost my confidence, I regret the many months I remained passive when I could have been practicing assertive communication. This is a trap you must avoid, especially if you think that people will only want to speak with you once you reach certain milestones.

Develop a Growth Mindset

Your growth mindset is so unlike the fixed mindset. With a fixed mindset, you accept your limitations—such as passiveness or a low IQ—and feel the need to get by in life with them. This means always taking the safest route around a perceptively dangerous situation. You also believe in the fallacy that says you've either got it or you haven't. If you believe that you've got the talent to lead a team of misfiring salesmen, then you'll apply your mind to the promotion on offer, something which Henry quite clearly didn't do when he applied for the promotion, he only applied because of pressure from his mother. So, right now I'd like you to take particular note of the following positive features of having a growth mindset:

- You are already an intelligent person and have the capacity to develop your intelligence still further.
- It does not matter if you are not yet able to address obstacles because you are nearly there, ready and willing to embrace challenges or setbacks.
- Your growth mindset doesn't take no for an answer and will continue to persist when you are dealing with setbacks, which, no matter what you may think of them, are an inevitable part of life.
- Over time, you will learn to develop a thick skin, not worrying about subjective comments from others, but learn from constructive criticism when given.
- You can ignore negative naysayers and those who tease you continuously and take whatever inspiration you can from the success of others who, invariably, will have their growth mindset to thank for their success.

Take the time to write these features down and repeat them to yourself, you'll be surprised how much it helps.

You'll encounter the concept of a growth mindset several times throughout this guide, and for good reason. It's an essential foundation for personal and professional development. Since I strongly encourage you to cultivate this mindset, here are some practical tips to help you build it into a lasting habit.

- **Recognize fixed mindset triggers** - Notice when you think of things like *"I'm just not good at this"* or *"I can't do it."* Remind yourself this doesn't reflect your new growth mindset.
- **Use "Yet" language** - *"I don't understand this... yet." "I haven't mastered it... yet."*
- **Embrace challenges** - Treat challenges as opportunities to grow, not as threats. When something is hard, remind yourself: *"This is how I learn."*
- **Learn from criticism and failure.** View feedback as useful, not personal. Ask: *"What can I learn from this?"*

Regular Self-Reflection

A big obstacle to developing a growth mindset and becoming an assertive man is not making a habit of self-reflection, or in fact not doing it at all. As you begin to make many changes to your life, it is vital that you regularly reflect on your thoughts, beliefs, and habits to see if what you are doing is actually worthwhile.

I hope the exercises in the first chapter have helped you understand why you are passive and the many ways you show it. But soon you will be taking action towards becoming an assertive man, therefore it is crucial you make a habit of regular self awareness, by journaling or other means, as is how you keep evidence that you are making progress.

Evidence is what brings us confidence. For example, if you dedicate 15 minutes each day to reading self-help dating books, and a month goes by and you still haven't approached a girl to ask out on a date due to lacking courage, you have created no real evidence of progress and you won't feel any more confident about yourself or your dating ability. Whereas, if instead you simply focused on taking action and tasked yourself to approach 3 attractive girls in a week asking for their number, even if you only managed to ask one girl, that is evidence.

Evidence is a valuable tool for feedback. In the early stages, it doesn't matter whether that evidence is positive or negative—what matters is that you're engaging with the process. Starting out can feel uncomfortable, but taking that first step is already progress. Now, you have something real to reflect on and learn from. If you choose not to regularly reflect on your actions, it makes building evidence much less effective, as you'll miss valuable insights hidden in your experiences. Without reflection, patterns go unnoticed, lessons are lost, progress slows and confidence stagnates.

Self-reflection doesn't need to be complicated. In fact, the key is to keep it simple. Trying to evaluate everything at once can quickly become overwhelming, which often leads to inaction. Instead, aim for consistency over complexity. You already have a list of the things that have caused you to build passive habits, pick just one root cause to focus on overcoming. For example, if fear of rejection is something that holds you back, dedicate a small amount of time each week to reflect on when you felt this fear, how you responded to it in the moment and what you could have done better.

One of the most effective tools for developing self-awareness, based on personal experience, is journaling. It's a cognitive technique that can help you process your thoughts, track your progress, and stay honest with yourself. Below is an example of how to carry out self-reflection when working through a fear, reframing a negative thought, or building (or breaking) a habit.

Week 1 – Facing Rejection

- **Goal:** Approach 3 women I find attractive and ask for their number.
- **Action Taken:** On Saturday night, I approached a woman at the bar who I found attractive. I told her I thought she was beautiful and asked for her number. She responded politely and said she had a boyfriend.
- **Positives:** I took action and confronted one of my biggest fears. The experience wasn't as uncomfortable as I had imagined. She appreciated the compliment and responded kindly.
- **Areas for improvement:** I only approached one woman, which fell short of my initial goal, but perhaps

my goal was too ambitious. I didn't get a number, but that's okay, it's part of the process. My body language was nervous and awkward, which I noticed in the moment.

- **Next Steps:** Set a more realistic goal to build confidence gradually. Focus on maintaining strong eye contact and slowing down my speech. Practice open, relaxed body language before going out. Consider doing some low-stakes social warm-ups before approaching someone I'm attracted to.

Week 2 – Working on Weaknesses

- **Goal:** Approach 2 women and ask for their number while maintaining confident body language and calm communication.

You get the idea...

Your journaling doesn't have to be exactly like that, you can write it however you like, the point is to just make a start, you can always build on it. Self awareness can also come from other people, they can reflect things back to you that you might not notice on your own, offering perspective, accountability, and encouragement. Sharing your self-reflection process with a trusted friend, mentor, or coach can deepen your understanding of yourself.

The key to meaningful self-improvement is creating a consistent loop of action and feedback. Set small, tangible goals that require real action, something you physically have to do, and then reflect on the outcome. You can't gather real evidence or make lasting change without engaging in the experience itself.

Finally, I am aware of the many different journalling exercises I have included in this guide, to keep it simple for yourself do the following. For daily journalling, stick to short, structured sessions like the morning journaling exercise in Chapter 4. For deeper reflection, set aside time each week for more focused progress tracking, this includes reviewing fears you've faced, reframing negative thoughts, breaking old passive habits, and reinforcing assertive behaviors. And as you begin to take action on the areas of your life you want to improve, be sure to reflect on those experiences as soon as you can afterward.

Misconceptions About Assertiveness

We've already explored one of the most common misconceptions about assertiveness, the tendency to confuse it with aggressiveness. This misunderstanding often causes people to shy away from assertive behavior out of fear it might damage their relationships with others. You might relate if you've assumed that being assertive would bring more trouble than benefit. This highlights how powerful misconceptions can be in holding you back from becoming the confident, assertive man you aspire to be. Therefore below is a list of the most common misconceptions, each of which debunked so that you shouldn't have any doubts going forward.

- *Because you are passive by nature, you cannot learn to be assertive.* This is a great example of the fixed mindset, by believing this misconception you accept your limitations and remain frustrated by not being able to get your needs met. Assertiveness is a skill that can be developed with practice, just like learning to play an instrument. It's all about striking the balance between standing up for yourself and respecting others, leading too far in each direction will either keep you passive or make you aggressive.

- *Assertive behavior is only practiced by extroverts.* Assertiveness is a communication style, not personality type, so while extroverts may be more outspoken, introverts can be just as assertive in their own way. Assertiveness is about expressing thoughts, needs, and boundaries clearly and respectfully, something that both introverts and extroverts can develop. Normally the case is that introverts prefer to communicate assertively through thoughtful conversation, written messages, or one-on-one discussions rather than in large social settings.
- *Being assertive means getting your way, not caring about how others may feel.* This is the case of confusing aggressive communication with assertive communication. True assertiveness is about balance, not dominance. Unlike aggression, which disregards others' perspectives, assertiveness encourages open and honest communication, fostering mutual understanding and cooperation. Which often leads to healthier relationships.

Steering Clear of Aggression

Months before taking on his role as the new supervisor, Chris was a nasty piece of work. His old aggressive habits meant that most of the time he got what he wanted, but at the expense of frustrating many of the workers, like Henry, and getting into a fair bit of trouble with his superiors. While you may want to always get your way, there are always consequences for when you don't do things the right way. Below is a list of aggressive behaviors so you know what to avoid.

- Yelling or shouting to intimidate or control a conversation.
- Interrupting constantly, talking over others or just not listening to what people have to say.
- Name-calling or using offensive labels. *"idiot," "useless."*
- Blaming others excessively without taking responsibility.
- Using threats. *"You'll regret this," "If you do that, you'll be sorry."*
- Criticizing harshly without constructive feedback.

- Making unfair accusations. *"You always mess things up."*
- Giving ultimatums rather than negotiating.
- Eye-rolling or exaggerated sighs to show disrespect.
- Aggressive hand gestures, like pointing fingers in someone's face.
- Slamming objects.
- Publicly humiliating a colleague for a mistake.
- Dismissing others' ideas rudely or without consideration.
- Taking credit for someone else's work.
- Dominating meetings and refusing to let others speak.
- Controlling behavior, like dictating what someone can wear or who they can see.
- Yelling during disagreements instead of discussing calmly.
- Threatening to leave or hurt oneself/others to manipulate a partner.
- Punishing with silence or emotional withdrawal.
- Criticizing or shaming a child or partner repeatedly.

Now of course, having been in and around boxing gyms for years, some of the behaviors above seem to be quite common. We sometimes can be slightly brutal as we joke around with each other, we try to get under each other's skin for a bit of a laugh but at the end of the day it is just a form of affection between good pals. So, there's nothing wrong with calling your mate an idiot or making up unfair accusations to wind them up. Just follow the rule, don't give out what you can't take. There is always a line. Especially, don't try this kind of banter with strangers, it will always come across as rude.

Breaking Down Your Barriers

So far, we've explored the idea that real change starts with you, emphasized the power of a growth mindset and regular self-awareness, and debunked some of the most common misconceptions about assertiveness. Now, it's time to get personal, and identify the specific barriers that are holding you back from taking action toward becoming more assertive.

One of the most significant barriers is fear.

In the first chapter, we discussed the root causes of passiveness, many of which still apply here. These underlying causes often show up as mental or emotional roadblocks that stop you from asserting yourself. In this section, we'll look at practical strategies and exercises to help you address these challenges directly. By now, you've likely begun to recognize the thoughts, patterns, or situations that keep you stuck in passive behavior. Let's take a closer look at some of the most common barriers people face, and how to start overcoming them.

Facing Fears

The fear of rejection, conflict, judgement and failure are the most common fears that passive people face. Henry could relate to all of them. One of the main reasons why he stood no chance of being promoted at work was because of his fear of *"ruffling feathers"* or *"rocking the boat"*. Having worked in sales long enough, he knew what was required to address the company's dismal performances from one quarter to the next. But he neither had the required thick skin or backbone to take remedial nor drastic action. He could not foresee himself in an influential role, making hard choices that subordinates would not like.

In life, success is often the result of consistently stepping outside of your comfort zone, as growth happens when you confront something unfamiliar or difficult, which triggers problem-solving, learning, and skill-building. The same applies for becoming assertive. By consistently pushing yourself into uncomfortable situations, whether it's approaching an attractive lady to get her number or stepping up to take the first penalty in a football match, you train your brain to handle pressure. Each attempt, whether successful or not, builds a valuable feedback loop: you either gain proof of your capability, or walk away with a lesson that fuels personal growth.

Just like Henry, I used to constantly worry about how others saw me. I was terrified of letting people down, it pushed me to become a perfectionist as I believed that if I made a small mistake, people would label me a failure and never forget it. But that mindset got knocked out of me, quite literally, after a few months of boxing training. I faced plenty of embarrassing moments in the gym, but not once did any of the other boxers hold it against me in a personal way. We all had our own awkward slip-ups and just laughed them off, and the more it happened, the less any of us cared about what others thought. That environment taught me to stop taking myself so seriously and motivated me to face my other fears.

Fear of rejection. The most common fear of all. Throughout my life I've been rejected countless times. Did it bother me then? Absolutely. Does it bother me now? Not at all. In fact, the more I was rejected, the less power it had over me. Looking back, I'm genuinely grateful that I took so many risks as a young man, even if they often ended in rejection, because those experiences shaped who I am today.

I've come to view rejection like money. If you only have $10 and lose $1, it feels significant, you've lost 10% of all you have. But if you have $1,000 and lose $1, it's barely noticeable. The more you experience rejection, the less each instance impacts you.

The simplest and most effective way to overcome your fear of rejection is to face it head-on: *get rejected*. It's not going to feel great at first, but with each experience, you build resilience. The more it happens, the better you become at handling it, and the less fear you'll have when taking future risks.

1. **Reframe rejection.** Rejection doesn't mean failure, it often just means something wasn't the right fit. It's not the end of the road, just a redirection. Most importantly, it's rarely personal. A rejection usually says more about the situation or the other party than it does about you.
2. **Normalize it.** Everyone experiences rejection, from job applications to relationships, even successful people that you look up to have been rejected countless times. It is a natural part of growth.

3. **Build desensitization.** Strengthen your rejection muscle by intentionally stepping into low-stakes situations where a no is possible. Ask for a discount, make an unexpected suggestion in a meeting, or try something new socially. Track your experiences, write down what you feared versus what actually happened. You'll likely find most rejections are far less painful than you imagined.
4. **Shift self-talk replace.** When facing a potential rejection, it's easy to spiral into negative thinking: *"What if they say no?"* Instead, reframe your inner dialogue: *"What if it goes well?" "Even if they say no, I'll be fine." "At least I had the courage to try."*

Fear of conflict. Conflict has been part of human nature since the dawn of time, whether it's a disagreement with your partner, political tension, or even full-scale war. It's certainly fair to say not all conflict is productive, but as a man, the worst thing you can do is avoid it altogether.

The goal isn't always to win, sometimes it's about finding a resolution. But in every case, stepping into conflict with courage and clarity is essential. Like rejection, the only way to get more comfortable with conflict is through experience. The more you face it, the more confident and composed you become.

1. **Understand the root.** Ask yourself: *"What am I really afraid of?"* Is it being disliked? Hurting someone's feelings? Losing control? Fear of conflict often stems from deeper issues, people-pleasing tendencies, past trauma, or the false belief that disagreement is inherently dangerous. Identifying the root cause gives you power over it.
2. **Redefine conflict.** Conflict isn't something to fear, it's a natural and necessary part of both personal and professional relationships. Think of it as collaboration under pressure. It's through conflict that differences are resolved, boundaries are clarified, and real growth takes place.
3. **Start small.** You don't have to dive into major confrontations right away. Begin by speaking up in low-stakes situations, a wrong food order, a scheduling mix-up, a minor disagreement. These moments build your confidence and help you develop the skill of managing discomfort rather than avoiding it.

Fear of judgement. No matter who you are or what you do, people will judge you. Not everyone will like you, agree with you, or understand you, and that's just life. With over 8 billion people in the world, all with different thoughts, emotions, and experiences, it's inevitable that someone, somewhere, will form a negative opinion about you. *So what?*

Their judgment doesn't define you, and it certainly doesn't make you any less of a man. Most of the time, you won't even know what people are thinking, and even if you did, it wouldn't change your worth. Here's the truth: Everyone worries about how they're perceived - yes, *everyone.* But most people are far too preoccupied with their own insecurities to scrutinize you the way you imagine. You're not under a spotlight. Most of the judgment you fear exists only in your head.

1. **Question your inner critic.** *Whose judgment am I really afraid of? A parent? Society? Strangers?* More often than not, it's not real people judging you, it's internalized voices from your past. When self-critical thoughts arise, pause and ask: *Is this thought kind? Is it true? Is it helpful?* If not, let it go.

2. **Practice vulnerability in safe places.** Start by sharing your thoughts, opinions, or creative work in low-risk environments. The goal isn't to be perfect, it's to get comfortable being seen. As you grow more confident, gradually increase your audience and push your edges.
3. **Expose yourself.** Lean into small, intentional acts that make you feel seen: post something online, speak up in a meeting, wear what you want, voice your opinion. Each time you do, the fear loses power. You'll often find that the imagined fear is far louder than the reality.

Fear of failure. This is closely tied to the fear of rejection, but it often cuts deeper, especially when it relates to our goals and aspirations. And there is something I can almost guarantee in your life...

You will fail.

It's essential. Failure is how we learn, adapt, and evolve. Every successful person has failed, many times. In fact, their success was built because of those failures. Nobody gets it right the first time. Nobody is perfect. And those who constantly chase perfection end up trapped in a cycle of frustration and self-doubt. Perfection is an illusion that keeps you stuck. Progress, on the other hand, is real, and it only comes through action, mistakes, and course correction. People who are too afraid to fail never take the risks necessary to grow.

1. **Redefine failure.** Failure isn't final, it's feedback. It's not a dead end, but a vital part of the learning process. Every successful person has failed, often more than once. The difference? They kept going. You should want to fail, but not repeat failures.
2. **Understand what exactly you are afraid of.** Humiliation? Disappointment? Letting someone down? Often, fear of failure is rooted in something deeper. When your fear is vague, it feels massive and unmanageable. But when you define it, you shrink it down to size, and it becomes something you can face.
3. **Break down the worst-case scenario**. *"What's the absolute worst that could happen?" "Could I handle that?" "What would I do if it did happen?"*

At the end of the day, the most important takeaway is simple: *do the thing you're afraid of*. Yes, it's easier said than done, but without that first step, you'll never discover what you're truly capable of. It's also worth understanding that some fears may never completely disappear. And that's okay. Even legends feel fear, Mike Tyson once admitted he felt *"scared to death"* in the lead up to the majority of his fights. He still put on a brave face and used that fear to enhance his performance.

Exercise 5 - Face Your Biggest Fear

You will now face your fears, but it can be overwhelming to take on everything at once. Choose your strongest fear of the four fears we've discussed: rejection, judgment, conflict and failure. Just one. That's enough for now. The goal is to gently expose yourself to situations that trigger real but manageable discomfort. You want to feel slightly stretched, not overwhelmed. This allows your brain to experience discomfort, survival, and recovery, rather than panic.

Use the exercise below as your guide. It's designed to help you build confidence gradually. The example provided focuses on the fear of judgment, but the same process applies to any fear you choose. Furthermore, what you may find is that just by facing one fear you begin to feel less intimidated by your other fears as you build proof that you can overcome it.

Step 1: Identify your fear and its cause. Write down the fear as clearly and honestly as possible and what you think may have caused you to develop that fear, whether it be past experiences, social conditioning or internal beliefs. *"I'm* *afraid of being judged because I think people will see me as awkward, not good enough, or unlikeable." "This fear started at school because I didn't fit in with the popular crowd and I was often made fun of."*

Step 2: Now your fear and its potential cause is written down, they don't matter anymore, they are left behind with the old version of yourself. Now you are going to take action, for this exercise to be effective you must repeat steps 2 (taking action) and 3 (reflecting on action) until you believe that your fear no longer holds power over you, or at least you have the courage to face this fear even if it still feels terrifying. Think of certain actions that link to your fear and break them down into steps, order them in ranking of how much you fear them, for example:

1. *Post an honest thought or opinion on social media. (Least Intimidating)*
2. *Share a personal story with a close friend.*
3. *Voice a different opinion during a group conversation.*
4. *Ask a question in a meeting or class, even if unsure.*
5. *Share creative work (writing, art, music) publicly.*

6. *Tell someone you respect that you're nervous or insecure about something.*
7. *Ask a stranger for the time or directions.*
8. *Ask a stranger for their honest opinion of your appearance. (Most Intimidating).*

Step 3: Work your way through the list, set yourself goals to regularly face those fears and reflect as soon as you can after taking action. Answer these questions in a journal or notes app:

1. *What did I do?*
2. *How anxious were you before, during, and after? (Rate each 0–10)*
3. *What did you expect to happen?*
4. *What actually happened?*
5. *Did I survive it? (Yes. Always yes.)*
6. *What did you learn about people's judgment, or your own expectations?*
7. *What would I do differently next time, if anything?*

Challenging Negative Beliefs

Henry has finally acted against his fears, although it took him a couple of weeks to carry out the plan he wrote down on his notepad, he has just taken a big step out of his comfort zone. For the first time in years, he joined his coworkers in the office cafeteria at lunch time. For as long as anyone could remember, Henry had claimed the corner desk like it was his personal fortress.

"Henry, are you lost?"

Though his coworkers were caught off guard, and joked about Henry not sitting in the corner, they still welcomed him over. It might sound like a small gesture, but for Henry, this was a huge breakthrough. He expected to be bullied off the table and laughed at, but instead he faced his strong fear of rejection that's been fueling his passive habits.

Unfortunately for Henry, the lunch break didn't go quite as he'd hoped. He sat in silence for most of the lunch break, feeling out of place. It reinforced a familiar, painful belief, that he was unimportant and didn't truly belong. In reality, no one at the table minded his presence. In fact, they were glad to see him step out of his usual corner. But because Henry didn't engage or express himself, he was left alone with his thoughts, interpreting silence as rejection.

Henry's negative beliefs twisted what should've been a powerful step forward into what felt like proof that he didn't belong. Instead of seeing courage, he saw confirmation that he should've never bothered trying. This goes to show how powerful your internal dialogue is.

Negative beliefs are thoughts or convictions you hold about yourself, others, or the world that are limiting, self-critical, or pessimistic. Such as *"I'm not good enough to get good grades at school,"* or *"Nobody wants me to play because I'm bad."* They often stem from past experiences, trauma, or social conditioning.

But that doesn't mean you can't overcome your negative beliefs, it just takes time. Yet again, taking repeated action is how you build evidence that your negative beliefs are irrational. It's all well and good setting yourself goals to take action, but real growth comes from following through, especially on the days you don't feel like it. That's how you build discipline and create a steady track record that proves you're far more capable than you once believed.

Even men who appear confident and successful on the outside still wrestle with self-doubt on the inside. The difference is, they've conditioned their minds to reframe negative thoughts and have built up enough experience to counter their inner critic. But for those who haven't developed those mental tools, negative beliefs can take hold, fueling passivity, lowering self-esteem, and distorting how they see themselves.

Put simply: if you keep telling yourself you're a loser, you'll start to feel like one. Your thoughts shape your reality. And when your inner dialogue is built on criticism and self-doubt, it's incredibly hard to build confidence or take risks.

Of course, it's not as simple as just *"stop thinking poorly of yourself."* If it were, therapists would be out of business. Overcoming self-doubt, low self esteem and reframing negative beliefs takes real work, self-awareness, and consistency. You have to consider the full picture: your past experiences, upbringing, environment, mental and physical health. These patterns don't change overnight. Like anything else, building great self-esteem comes from developing healthy habits. We'll dive deeper into that in the next chapter. But for now, the first step is to begin challenging those negative beliefs, because if you don't question them, they'll continue to define you.

The more you challenge the negative things you believe about yourself, the closer you get to accepting your so-called "flaws" for what they really are, just parts of being human. You have to consider that there are aspects of yourself you can't, and don't need to, change. You don't have to reinvent yourself to feel confident or accepted. The more you embrace who you truly are, the less pressure you feel to pretend around others. For instance, if you're naturally introverted, you don't need to be the loudest voice in the room to feel good about yourself. You might simply thrive in smaller, more meaningful settings. Perhaps your needs might actually involve maintaining a low profile. It's about learning to say no to things that don't serve you, such as big social events, and intentionally placing yourself in situations where you can thrive, like quiet get-togethers with close friends. Yet again, it all relates to your needs.

Exercise 6 - Act Against Your Negative Beliefs

But there is still work to be done on addressing your passive behavior. Even if life feels unfair or like you're always going to struggle, you still have power. You can plan your day, take things one step at a time, and keep moving toward the kind of man you want to become. And maybe the most important part is just starting. Being honest about your core beliefs, both the good and the bad, is worth it. Try this deep self reflection journaling exercise to really understand and begin to reframe your negative beliefs.

1. **Identify your negative beliefs.** Off the top of your head, write down the list of negative beliefs that pop into your head on a daily basis. Examples include: *"I'm not good enough." "I don't deserve love" "I always mess things up." "I'll never get better." "I'm weak if I ask for help." "I don't matter to others."*
2. **Notice when a negative belief is active.** Of the list of your negative beliefs, link them to specific scenarios where you tend to feel anxious or defeated. You may think *"I'm too awkward"* or *"They will think I'm strange"* when you briefly make eye

contact with a stranger, causing you to panic and awkwardly look at the floor. Ensure your list of your negative beliefs is linked to the activating event.

3. **Identify the source.** Many of our negative beliefs were shaped by early life experiences, trauma, or repeated messages from our environment. These could be things such as receiving emotional abuse from parents, being bullied at school, or being told that if you show your emotions you are weak. Next to each of your beliefs and activating events, try to link the source, or sources, of your passiveness next to them.

   a. For example, belief: *"I always mess things up,"* root cause: repeated criticism from a parent or teacher for small mistakes, message learned: *"Mistakes are unacceptable. If I fail, I am a failure,"* passive behavior: *"I'll play it safe, or won't try so I don't mess up."*

4. **Look for evidence against the belief.** Ask yourself: *When have I proven this belief wrong? What strengths do I have that contradict this thought? What do others say about me that challenges this belief?* For example, evidence against

"I'll never get better" could be receiving good grades at school, seeing progress at the gym or simply having good friends.

5. **Reframe the thought**. *"I always screw things up."* -> *"I've made mistakes, but I've also learned and grown. I'm improving."* You can also write this down to help interrupt the automatic thought loop going on in your brain and see it more objectively.

6. **Act against the belief**. Your actions can challenge your beliefs more powerfully than thought alone. *Afraid you're awkward?* Start conversations with strangers about anything. *Think you're incompetent?* Take on small, achievable tasks and reflect on the wins. Behavior creates real-world evidence that the belief is false.

7. **Regular self reflection**. This is a very common theme in this guide, but the reason why it's repeated so much is because of how important it is. Make a regular habit of reviewing your actions when challenging your negative beliefs by asking yourself these questions:

a. What exactly is the belief I'm holding right now and what triggers it?
b. Is this belief rational and what belief would serve me better right now?
c. What action can I take to help take on a better belief?
d. (After taking action) Did my action reinforce my irrational belief, or challenge it? If it reinforced the belief, in what way?
e. Was taking the action better or worse than I thought it would be?
f. What can I do to make my actions more effective in challenging and reshaping this irrational belief in the future?

Changing your mindset requires a lifelong commitment to continuous trial and error, that's why you must stay on top of these habits.

Finally, I want to highlight one of the biggest mistakes I made during my transformation journey: the *"I don't need any help, I can do it all on my own"* mindset. While I respect the desire to protect your reputation and appear strong, I've been there, and I can tell you from experience, it only made things harder for no good reason. Here's the truth: asking for help doesn't make you weak. In fact, people don't think any less of you when you reach out, in many cases, they actually respect you more. Most importantly, many people want to help. It gives them a sense of purpose and connection. So when you ask, it's not just helping you, it's often a win-win.

Breaking Passive Habits

While I want you to keep referring to yourself as an assertive man, the truth is that you're still showing signs of passivity, and it will take months or maybe years of consistent effort to fully make that transition. This isn't to discourage you, I simply want you to understand the importance of habits and how they form your identity.

The reason you are passive is because you've repeated a wide range of passive behaviors regularly, usually in situations that make you uncomfortable, until your brain wired them in as your automatic response. Over time, your passive responses have solidified into habits, and your habits shape your identity.

The saying goes: you are what you repeatedly do.

Habits are automatic behaviors or routines that we do regularly, often without thinking. They're formed through repetition and become part of our daily rhythm, like brushing your teeth, checking your phone, or drinking water after waking up. Or maybe for you, showing signs of nervousness when an attractive lady walks into the room.

If you run 4 times a week, people would consider you a runner. If you show signs of nervousness in group discussions, people would consider you socially awkward. It's that simple. So in order to change from passive to assertive, you need to break passive habits and build assertive ones, and this is done by understanding and changing the habit loop.

1. **Cue** (The Trigger) - This is the signal that kicks off the habit loop. It tells the brain something is happening and it should respond. For example, when a socially awkward man arrives at a friend's gathering in which he doesn't know everybody there, when he notices strangers talking confidently, laughing and making

eye contact, it sets off his cue of feeling anxiety: *"I don't feel like I belong here."*

Event Occurs -> Brain Senses Potential Discomfort

2. **Craving** (The Desire) - A craving is not about the behavior itself, it's about the internal feeling the behavior promises to resolve. Cravings are the emotional drivers behind every habit. He craves relief from social discomfort, fear of embarrassment, or rejection. It's not that he wants to avoid people. He wants to feel safe, in control, and not judged. So, his brain associates withdrawal or staying silent with emotional protection. *"If I stay quiet, I won't mess up."*

Brain Signals that Event Could Bring Emotional Discomfort -> Sets Off Craving of Emotional Protection

3. **Response** (The Behavior) - This is the action you take to satisfy the craving, triggered by the cue. He avoids eye contact, stays quiet, maybe checks the weather app on his phone, or physically moves away

from the group. This is his habitual response to emotional discomfort.

Brain Craves Emotional Protection -> Triggers Behavior that Prevents Emotional Discomfort

4. **Reward** (The Outcome) - The reward is what teaches the brain whether this behavior is worth repeating. Even if the reward is short-term, it creates a loop of reinforcement. He feels a temporary sense of relief: no awkward moments, no risk of rejection, no spotlight. The brain says, *"That worked—do it again next time."*

Safe Behavior Carried Out for the Duration of Event -> Brain Gains Feedback that Behaving that Way Prevents Emotional Discomfort

Exercise 7 - Redesign Your Habit Loop

Now it is time to break these habits, and you will do so by reprogramming your habit loop. This involves consciously interrupting each stage and inserting intentional alternatives. Below, you'll find a step-by-step guide to help you rewire your habit patterns, followed by an example illustrating how the previously discussed *"awkward man"* could apply these steps to overcome passivity in a social setting. Using both the instructions and example, I expect you to create your own plan to break your passive habits.

- **Make it invisible**. This means disrupting the cue that begins your passive habit. To do this you can remove triggers from your environment. Out of sight, out of mind. *Example:* If you tend to avoid speaking up during meetings because you sit in the back and stay unnoticed, try changing your environment by sitting closer to the front or near more engaged participants.
- **Make it unattractive**. This means to weaken the craving. Reframe how you think about the habit so it no longer feels appealing. *Example:* If your passive habit is staying quiet to *"keep the peace,"* remind

yourself that avoiding difficult conversations often leads to resentment, missed opportunities, and feeling invisible.

- **Make it difficult**. This means to block the response. Increase friction between you and the habit. Increase the effort required to do it. *Example:* If you often let others make decisions for you in social situations, like where to eat or what to do, make it harder to default to *"I don't mind"* by committing to offering at least one suggestion ahead of time.
- **Make it unsatisfying**. This means to undermine the reward. Add immediate consequences or remove the pleasure. *Example:* If you tend to avoid speaking up during conversations, create accountability by asking a friend or coach to check in with you afterward. If you stayed passive, you report it—and possibly reflect on the missed opportunity. Knowing someone is watching increases the discomfort of remaining silent.

Invisible Cue. The initial cue of *"I don't feel like I belong here."* needs to be reframed as a signal for growth, rather than danger. Sticking with the socially awkward man at a social gathering, he can begin to use a mental script or mantra such as *"Discomfort means I'm growing,"* each time he enters a social setting.

To make the cue of your passive habit become invisible, you need to be aware of the events that trigger your passive habits. However that is easier said than done, especially if you have a lot on your mind. Use the two tips below to help maintain great self awareness.

- Use visual reminders - Type in reminders of affirmations on your phone that shows the assertive alternative to your passive thoughts. For example, you can set reminders to pop up on your phone when you're at a social event, such as *"Introduce yourself, people want to get to know you."*
- Change your environment - You simply cannot develop your communication skills if you choose to isolate yourself from everybody. Make it a goal of yours to leave the house more, join clubs/communities and partake in group discussions at work. He doesn't know it, but the awkward man is already doing this by actually turning up to the social gathering.

Unattractive Craving. His initial craving that he is safe if he stays invisible needs to be made unattractive. He needs to understand his craving of *"I want to feel safe,"* will only keep him rooted in passiveness, furthermore he could visualize a life in which he never breaks his passive habits and faces the consequences such as unhealthy relationships, a lack of human connection and forever staying the awkward man he doesn't like being.

He can then begin to create a positive craving by reframing how he thinks about the habit. Instead of focusing on what is being given up, comfort, safety, or familiar patterns, focus on what is being gained: confidence, clarity, progress.

Difficult Response. He can add extra difficulty in following through with his passive behaviors, such as withdrawal, silence, and checking his phone constantly, by increasing the effort it takes to engage in them. For example, he could leave his phone at home or keep it tucked away in his bag to prevent the urge to check it. Additionally, if he catches himself zoning out or drifting to the edges of the crowd, he could intentionally move closer to where conversations are happening to encourage interaction.

He could then attempt to change his passive behaviors to low-stakes social action such as: Making brief eye contact with someone and introducing himself, asking a stranger a simple question like *"How was your weekend?"*, or smiling and reacting to a group conversation nonverbally. Replace avoidance with tiny connection efforts. Simplify the response, or the action itself. This is where most people go wrong, they try to do too much, too soon.

Unsatisfying Reward. His current passive habit offers short-term relief from discomfort and social risk, but this relief comes at a cost: missed opportunities, disconnection, and lingering self-doubt. To make his passive reward less appealing, he needs to consciously reframe it as a trap that keeps him stuck, not safe. He could even set up an agreement with his friend that each time he checks his phone at a social event out of awkwardness, he has to pay him $1, like a fine system.

He could then replace it with a more meaningful and lasting reward: a sense of pride, momentum, and real emotional safety through genuine engagement. He can reinforce assertive behavior by recognizing his effort immediately after it happens: *"I stayed present, that's a win."* By tracking his progress, he is building evidence that he is no longer an awkward, passive man.

Now it's your turn. The key is to keep it simple. Return to your list of passive habits and choose just one to break. It will be uncomfortable and challenging, but it will absolutely be worth it. Finally, it's important to mention that building healthy habits often means doing the opposite of the 4 steps above. Below are the 4 prompts on how to do this, inspired by the excellent book *Atomic Habits* by James Clear.

Cue: Make it obvious.

Craving: Make it attractive

Response: Make it easy.

Reward: Make it satisfying.

4. The Importance of Habits

I think naturally, if you're an actor, there's a high level of assertiveness that you need to have to survive this business. There's boldness in being assertive, and there's strength and confidence. –Bryan Cranston

In many ways, Henry could relate to what Walter White put himself through. On his fiftieth birthday, surrounded by loving friends and family, White had to wonder to himself: *What have I achieved in this short life of mine, now more than halfway to its inevitable end?* Like Henry, White was as passive as they came. As a high school science teacher, his students could never take his enthusiasm for the subject seriously. Walter White couldn't get these disinterested kids to pay attention and discipline themselves to do well.

It gave the high school teacher no joy in failing his students. He feared what they thought of him. He lacked the confidence that could help him emulate the inspirational heights reached by Mr. Chips, a British public school teacher, second to none. Like Mr. Chips, Mr. White, the hapless

American high school teacher with no interest in school sports and other physical activities that would usually endear a devoted teacher to his testosterone-enriched male students, is a fictional character.

He is not a figment of my imagination. He is the protagonist in the ground-breaking, award-winning TV series *Breaking Bad*, played by US actor Bryan Cranston. It is the story of a down-on-his-luck high school teacher who turns to the dangerous world of drug dealing not just to make ends meet but to elevate his self-esteem. That White goes about it in the wrong way-never mind that what he is doing is illegal-is where this acclaimed serialized story becomes interesting.

Like Henry's behavior toward his mother, White appeared to get his way with ruthless antagonists by resorting to passive-aggressive behavior, which, of course, got him into more trouble instead of helping him. Over time, White's attempts at aggression and machismo would backfire on him.

Now three months have passed since the promotion, Henry has started to take concrete steps to confront the many fears that have kept him stuck in passivity. He's gradually learning that, even when well-intentioned, other people's opinions shouldn't define his sense of self. Still, he lacks real-life experiences that would serve as proof of his growth into a more assertive man, there's still much work ahead.

For the time being, he needs to prioritize his personal needs. This means learning to start saying no to many of the Dicks, Toms, and Harrys that always seem to cross his path, no matter how much he tries to avoid them.

Saying no to peer pressure and other men's unreasonable demands still rankles Henry, he tends to take on additional tasks at work with no real benefit. While he has made some progress - instead of continuing to live his life according to his mother's wishes, he began respectfully asking for less input, explaining that he wanted to live on his own terms. He's even started looking at apartments to move into.

But, he still finds it difficult to deal with confrontation. Henry wants to earn the kind of respect that assertive men seem to command effortlessly, but first he must learn how to respect himself.

Respect Yourself

The old adage says that respect goes a long way. They also say that respect is earned, but if you feel as though you haven't achieved much in your life so far, do not let these affirmations overwhelm you and deter you from your passive to assertive transformation. Also, letting people walk all over you, especially those you're scared of or feel pressured by, isn't how you respect yourself. While Chris continues to make great strides as a workplace leader, he continues to rely on his steadfast belief that it is better to be feared than respected.

A few hours after Henry's bold decision to sit with the others at lunch, he found himself back at his desk, pen in hand, reflecting. *How do I get the others to notice me at the table?* No one had been openly rude or dismissive, but the lack of effort to include him in the conversation felt like quiet rejection. At least, that's how it felt at the moment.

But thanks to his habit of journaling, Henry was starting to recognize these old patterns of thinking. It wasn't really about them, it was about him. The problem wasn't a lack of respect from others; it was that Henry had not yet learned to respect himself.

Following this, Henry began researching all the male role models he looked up to: men who exuded confidence, earned respect effortlessly, and seemed to be genuinely admired by those around them. *What were they doing that he wasn't?*

It didn't take long for patterns to emerge. They all took their physical health very seriously, hitting the gym with discipline and consistency. They spoke clearly and confidently, introducing themselves without hesitation. They worked hard, carried themselves with purpose, and lived by a set of strong, healthy routines.

So, if you want to become more assertive, more respected, and more self-assured, you have to start by replacing your old, unhealthy, passive habits with new ones that reflect the kind of person you aspire to be. Let's explore what those habits are, and how to make them stick.

Healthy Habits to Begin With

The goal of this guide is to not just give you advice on how to assert yourself in various conversations, but to help you build habits that over time shift your identity from a passive to assertive person. So, firstly, I recommend you start every morning with a simple journaling exercise. The morning is when your mind is fresh, this clarity of thought, also laced with levels of optimism not always taken note of, could set you up to face the rest of the day with high levels of resilience. For this journaling exercise simply write down the following:

1. Write 1–2 sentences about your current emotional state.
2. Write your top 3 priorities for today, things you want to accomplish, big or small.
3. Write one thing you're grateful for.
4. Write one thing you'll do for yourself today. Self-care, a break, something joyful.

Starting your day with the right habits can boost your mood, energy, and focus. That's why your next habit is to build a simple morning routine, something that sets you up to feel good and stay on track for the rest of the day.

1. Begin your day with the journaling exercise discussed.
2. Light exercise - such as a 10 minute walk.
3. Personal hygiene - shower, grooming, skincare.
4. Breakfast - keep it healthy and replenish electrolytes.
5. Mindfulness - 5 minute box breathing exercise.

Now your start to every day is sorted, let's discuss habits for any time of the day. A great habit for when you are getting a bit hot under the collar, you could meditate. There is nothing imposing about this age-old practice. You do not need to meditate like a guru in order to create a sense of peace and calm. All it might need is just 30 seconds of deep, relaxed breathing to bring you down to earth.

Let's return to Henry. What did his years of isolation in the far corner of the office cafeteria teach us? That retreating into solitude didn't protect him, it only made things worse. By avoiding interaction, he gave his negative beliefs room to grow unchecked, like a parasite feeding on his self-worth. Over time, those thoughts shaped a passive personality that kept him feeling "safe" from rejection and judgment, but at a cost.

Therefore a habit for you to build is to keep yourself close to others. Also, rely on them for feedback. Perhaps if your challenges feel overwhelming, ask peers for advice. Spending more time in the company of others should also help you to pull yourself out of the habit of negative self-talk. No matter how introverted you think you may be, as humans we all crave social interaction, so if you have problems weighing down on your mind, make it a habit to share your thoughts with those that you trust. A problem shared is a problem halved.

Visualization is another great habit for becoming assertive. Start small by visualizing each day where you see yourself in the future. Before planning ahead, plan your day, but keep your plans real. They must be achievable. Write out these visualizations if it helps. Creating a daily to-do list can help you remain productive. Examples of this could include: *"Speak up at least once during class discussion"*, *"Politely say 'no' if I'm asked to do something that overwhelms me"*, or *"Practice making eye contact and using a firm but friendly voice when I talk"*.

Always remember the basics. Habits of regular exercise, healthy eating, quality sleep, personal hygiene, time management, lifelong learning and finance are essential for a healthy, balanced, and productive life. To ensure that you stay mentally strong enough to challenge the irrational beliefs that are keeping you passive, make a habit of the following:

- Complete some kind of exercise for at least 30 minutes every day.
- Limit sitting and screen time, or introduce regular breaks.
- Drink at least 2 liters of water a day.
- Eat balanced meals high in protein, with fruit and vegetables.
- Limit junk food or foods high in sugar.
- Aim for 7-9 hours of sleep each night.
- Set yourself a regular bed time and alarm for the morning.
- Avoid using screens an hour before bed.

- Shower, brush teeth, floss and wash hands frequently.
- Prioritize tasks and create to-do lists.
- Read regularly - try 15 minutes a day.
- Reflect on your mistakes and grow from them - journal.
- Attempt to save 20-50% of what you earn each month.
- Avoid impulse purchases.

Developing Self-Esteem

Building lasting self-esteem takes time, often months or even years of consistent effort. But that doesn't mean you have to wait years to start feeling better about yourself. The moment you begin working on your self-worth, your life can start to improve. Developing your self-esteem means recognizing your value, embracing your strengths, and learning from setbacks without harsh self-judgment. With strong self-esteem, you're better equipped to set healthy boundaries, pursue your goals with resilience, and maintain a positive mindset, even in difficult times.

While passive habits can keep you stuck in rigid patterns, setting healthy boundaries is something entirely different. It's not about building walls to shut the world out, it's about creating space where you can grow and thrive. Cognitively speaking, the most effective way to break old habits is to replace them with new habits.

Building self esteem is a personal journey, therefore you cannot let what others may think of you get to you. You will be making many changes to your life and, of course, people will have things to say. Focus, instead, on respecting yourself. To begin the process of asserting yourself internally, practice the following habits:

- **Surround yourself with positive people.** Align yourself with people who could be a positive influence on you during those times when you are still struck dumb with doubt and indecision. To go about doing this, aim to spend less time with those who belittle you. Join groups or clubs with shared interest, a running club is a great way to maintain fitness and find people with similar goals.
- **Do the things that bring you joy.** Life is way too short to constantly stick to difficult routines, while

they are important for building self-esteem and achieving goals, it's equally important not to lose sight of what makes life enjoyable. On occasion, let go of the schedule. Do something simply because you love it, whether it be meeting up with friends, playing golf on a Sunday or watching a TV series. Just don't see this as an excuse to drop the healthy habits you are currently building. Find a balance that works for you.

- **Practice self-compassion.** Treat yourself with kindness rather than harsh self-criticism. Everyone makes mistakes, it's an inevitable part of being human. Instead of endlessly replaying an embarrassing moment or dwelling on regret, remind yourself: *"I made the best choice I could with the awareness I had at the time."* This simple act of self-compassion helps you release the weight of self-blame.
- **Set achievable goals**: Start with small, realistic goals and celebrate your progress. Success builds confidence. It can be as simple as setting yourself a goal of introducing yourself to 3 new people each time you go out. You can build on your goals as you progress.

- **Focus on your strengths**: Make a list of your positive qualities, talents, and accomplishments. For example, you could be in good shape which shows you are very disciplined. Reflect on these often. Furthermore, reflect on how you developed these strengths, surely if you have managed to become great at many other skills then what's stopping you from becoming an assertive man?
- **Avoid comparisons**: Comparison is the thief of joy. Everyone's journey is unique. Focus on your own growth instead of measuring yourself against others. Social media often shows only the highlights, successes, vacations, filtered photos, not the struggles behind the scenes. Comparing your real life to someone else's curated version can steal your joy and distort your self-worth. So it's always a good idea to limit social media use.
- **Limit distractions**. Try to avoid things like excessive social media or mindless entertainment as they pull your attention away from the activities that actually build self-worth, such as setting and achieving goals, learning new skills, or reflecting on personal values.

Some more wisdom from myself here: At one stage in my self-improvement journey, I made the mistake of isolating myself from society for almost a year, what many call monk mode. During that time, I was laser-focused on discipline. I stuck to healthy habits, made great progress in fitness, and poured myself into learning and creating. On paper, it looked productive. But in reality, I lacked something essential: a life.

A great life isn't just built on productivity, it's built on a wide variety of experiences, relationships, and memories. When I look back on those 10–11 months, what do I really have to remember beyond workouts, research, and output? I had very little to show in terms of human connection or shared moments.

When I finally went back to normal life, it felt strange. I struggled to connect, had little to talk about, and realized I hadn't nurtured any friendships. My social confidence had taken a hit, and I had to relearn how to interact comfortably again.

Balance is key. Discipline and focus are important, but so are connection, joy, and presence. You can't build social confidence in isolation, and you can't grow into an assertive, well-rounded person without engaging with the world. Self-improvement shouldn't come at the cost of your humanity. Furthermore, you physically need to socialize in order to become an assertive individual!

I hope this encourages you to take action, especially on the things that make you nervous or uncertain. In my experience, the moments that once filled me with anxiety often turned into some of my best memories. When you're old and grey, it's the rich catalog of experiences you'll cherish, not just the sheer amount of output you achieved in whatever you do, or the digits in your bank account.

Exercise 8 - Practice Being a Better You

For this exercise, you are going to begin to prioritize your goals as it allows you to honor what truly matters to you. Start by identifying your most important goals, whether they're related to your career, relationships, health, personal growth, or passions. Once you know what you want to achieve, organize your time and energy around these priorities instead of getting distracted by less meaningful tasks or other people's expectations. Follow the steps below.

- **Step 1:** Write down 3–5 specific goals that matter most to you right now. These can be related to any area of your life. For example: *Read one personal development book every month to expand my knowledge and improve my mindset.*
- **Step 2:** For each goal, write a short sentence explaining why it's important to you. This will help keep you motivated and focused. *"Building a habit of regular reading will keep me on a path of continuous learning which will help develop many skills and prepare me for further education."*

- **Step 3:** Break each goal down into small, manageable tasks to make progress more achievable and less overwhelming. For instance, instead of trying to read an entire book at once, set a clear daily target like *"reading 15 pages a day and taking notes."*
- **Step 4:** Write down specific times in your calendar for working on these tasks. Treat these appointments as non-negotiable.
- **Step 5:** Identify activities or commitments that don't support your goals. Practice saying "no" or reduce time spent on these to protect your energy. Removing your gaming console from your room will encourage more thorough reading sessions.
- **Step 6:** Keep a journal, checklist, or use an app to record when you complete tasks. Seeing your progress builds momentum and confidence.
- **Step 7:** Take time to acknowledge and reward yourself for every step forward, no matter how small.
- **Step 8:** Once a week or month, revisit your goals and tasks. Adjust them as needed based on what's working or changing in your life. You could increase your daily reading task from 15 to 20 pages a day.

When working towards goals, it's important to practice constant goal setting by regularly reviewing and adjusting your objectives to stay aligned with your evolving priorities and progress. If you stick with the same goal without gradually increasing its challenge, you risk stagnating as growth comes from pushing yourself. At the same time, avoiding burnout is crucial, balancing hard work with rest, self-care, and realistic expectations prevents exhaustion.

Speak Like You Mean It

Cogito, ergo sum-Descartes

The Latin c*ogito, ergo sum*, usually translated into English as *"I think, therefore, I am,"* is the first principle of René Descartes's philosophy. But for the purposes of my self-empowerment exercise, I turned his statement on its head, revising it to *I feel, therefore, I am*. In other words, this is how I am feeling today, and what am I going to do about it? So that they don't stand in my way, I also had to take into account the behavior of some of my peers who could never seem to take no for an answer.

But before I could effectively project myself towards others, I first had to check my own needs. People, particularly those who always seem to want to find a reason to disagree with you, can see this indecisive feature of passive behavior a mile off and won't hesitate to take advantage of this.

Understanding Your Needs

The thing that intrigued me about Descartes' statement was his use of the *"I"* statement. It turned out to be significant because it goes to the root of how you need to assert yourself toward others. I want to reiterate that by putting yourself in the spotlight and expressing what you need others to understand about your needs, you are not being selfish. To my mind, conservative use of the *"I"* statement forms an important part of your boundaries being seen to work.

Understanding your needs allows you to make informed decisions about your life. Let's be honest, without a need there's no real reason to do anything. Until you have made up your mind, how can you actually force yourself to go out there and get it? To pluck up the courage to speak to an attractive girl, you need to find her attractive and want to build a relationship with her. To ask your boss for a promotion, you need to be willing to take on extra responsibility and want a higher salary. Typically speaking, the people with the most hunger get the most success in life. Cristiano Ronaldo is a great example.

What do you actually want from life?

A better relationship with family and friends? A higher paying job? People to stop walking over you? The list goes on, I am sure by now after all the self reflection and action you have carried out, you are well aware of what you want.

To get what you want you need to set boundaries, it does not mean that you are building a wall around yourself to shut yourself off from potential interpersonal conflict; it means that you are asserting yourself. It is the simple act of saying no to beers and pizza after work because you want to be in great shape for the summer holidays.

You are also standing up for yourself. Life is too short to take grief from other people. For example, as an assertive man, you will have no issue explaining your frustration to your condescending supervisor at work. In a respectful manner, of course.

A better understanding of your needs will also help you to communicate better with others, thus contributing towards the creation of better relationships with others, as well as creating a happier and more fulfilling life for yourself. To do a personal needs analysis, work your way through the following steps:

- **Brainstorm your needs.** Grab a pen and paper and list every need or desire you have, big or small, serious or lighthearted. Don't filter or judge; just get everything down.
- **Write the outcome of getting each need met.** Next to each need, write how having it fulfilled would improve your life. Then, rate each one on a scale from 1 to 10 based on how urgent or important it feels right now.
- **Prioritize your needs.** Create a new list, this time organizing your needs in order of importance. This helps you stay focused on what truly matters and gives you the motivation to communicate assertively and take action.
- **Regularly Reflect.** Your needs may shift over time. Review your list monthly to update priorities or remove what no longer applies. If you've fulfilled certain needs, note the results and how satisfied you feel.

Creating Boundaries

Understanding your needs is the key to creating and maintaining meaningful boundaries. As mentioned earlier, without a clear *"why,"* it's hard to stay committed to any action. The advice and examples below will guide you through the fundamentals of creating boundaries that not only protect your well-being but also empower you to communicate your needs openly and confidently.

Once you've identified a specific need, the next step is to translate that into a clear and practical boundary. This is what protects your need in real-life situations. Your boundary should be: *Specific* - not vague or open-ended, *Actionable* - something you can uphold or enforce, and *Respectful* - assertive, not aggressive. Below are some examples.

- Need: *I need to feel emotionally safe in my relationships.* Boundary: *"I will not stay in relationships where I am emotionally abused."*
- Need: *I need space to process my emotions.* Boundary: *"I'm not ready to talk right now, I'll come back to this when I've had time to think."*

- Need: *I need downtime after work to recharge.* Boundary: *"I won't schedule social plans on weeknights."*
- Need: *I need to be treated with respect in conversations.* Boundary: *"If you keep interrupting me, I won't speak to you."*

I can't provide specific boundaries for every possible need, so it's important that you take a closer look at your own needs and consider how you can translate each one into a healthy, supportive boundary. A great formula for creating boundaries:

"When [this happens], I will [action]".

Expressing Your Needs With Conviction

Now that you've identified your boundaries and have a solid understanding of your needs, the next step is to protect them through assertive communication. Most of the time this is the hardest part, because other people like to make it difficult for you to say no.

Let's say you've promised your family that you'll stay in this weekend to focus on your health, and spend quality time together. But then, just as you're settling in, the boys show up at your door and suddenly transform into persuasive masterminds. Next thing you know, they're throwing around a mix of cheeky insults and harmless threats, all aimed at getting you down to the pub. Here, I'm speaking from plenty of experience. Many times I went from a firm *"no"* to *"okay I'll just have one..."*

Anyway, as an assertive man, you need to be able to express your needs clearly and confidently. That means being firm when it matters. In fact, the stronger your needs are, the more important it becomes to stand your ground. When you're just getting started, it can be difficult to prioritize your own needs because you're often accustomed to putting others first.

I remember how awkward and intimidating it felt when I first started asserting myself.

Take Henry, for example. He's now at a point where he understands his needs and has even put some boundaries in place; he no longer wants to take on extra work at the office that offers no real benefit to him. The problem is, he struggles to communicate that clearly. He hesitates, lacks conviction, and as a result, he eventually gives in to the office bullies. But he is still learning and so are you, below are tips on how to communicate or express your needs effectively.

1. **Be clear and direct**: Say what you need without over-explaining or apologizing. Don't beat around the bush. *"I really enjoyed our date together, I'd like to see you again next Saturday."* Clarity avoids confusion and sets expectations without leaving room for misinterpretation.

2. **Use "I" statements:** Focus on your feelings and needs, not the other person's behavior. *"I know I'm new to this job, but I don't like it when you speak to me like I'm an idiot. I would appreciate it if you spoke to me just like you do everybody else"* It keeps the conversation non-confrontational and centered on your experience.

3. **Stay calm and grounded**. Even if the other person reacts emotionally, stay firm and respectful. *"I understand you may be upset, but I cannot help you with this right now because I'm busy, maybe I can

help another time." Maintaining composure reinforces your boundaries and prevents escalation.

4. **Anticipate pushback.** People will test your boundaries, expect it and stay consistent. If someone keeps asking you to help on their project after you've already told them many times you can't, don't be afraid to let them know that they are being pushy and always stick to your guns. Repetition and consistency show that your boundaries aren't negotiable.

5. **Say no without guilt**. Decline without justifying or trying to please. *"No thanks, I'm not interested."* It shows self-respect and teaches others to respect your time and energy too.

6. **Validate yourself first.** Remind yourself that your needs are valid, even if others don't understand them. *"I'm allowed to take care of myself without feeling guilty."* Inner confidence helps you express your needs more assertively. Always put yourself first, because in this cruel world not many people are going to put you first.

7. **Be honest, not harsh.** You can be firm and kind at the same time. *"I really value our time together, but I also need regular space to decompress."* Honesty builds mutual understanding without damaging relationships.

Finally, if setting boundaries feels unfamiliar, start small by saying no to the things you usually agree to out of guilt. Use daily journaling to track how these small boundaries make you feel, helping you gradually build the confidence to establish the boundaries that truly matter to you. Remember, setting boundaries is a practice, no one has the right to be upset when you stand up for yourself, and if they are, that reflects on them, not you.

Listening Actively

After a couple months of regular self-reflection and ongoing learning through self-help guides, Henry has come to realize that his previous communication style at the office often came across as disrespectful, despite not meaning to offend. Now he can see why certain people weren't too keen on him. From this point on he is committed to showing respect to everybody he speaks with, he is actively working on improving how he interacts with others, beginning with practicing active listening. Here are some key skills he's focusing on:

- Pay close attention to what the other person is saying, especially if they hold a senior position or are older. Showing genuine respect means valuing their perspective, regardless of your initial feelings.
- Maintain consistent eye contact, avoid interrupting, and stay mentally present throughout the conversation. Even if the topic feels dull, showing engagement through nods or thoughtful questions signals respect and openness. Asking clarifying questions helps show you care about their message.
- While you have every right to disagree, especially when you can provide evidence rather than assumptions, hold back immediate judgment. Approach disagreements with empathy, focusing on ideas and potential solutions instead of criticizing the person.
- When it's your turn to speak, choose your words carefully. Acknowledge the other person's emotions

and perspectives before sharing your own thoughts. This approach helps keep the conversation constructive and respectful.
- When someone is opening up or expressing intense emotions, be ready to offer both space and support, sometimes simply being a compassionate presence is more valuable than trying to fix the problem. Especially with women, it can often be more helpful to listen attentively and show that you truly understand, rather than immediately offering solutions.

Thinking back to the time I spent with my folks, my mother did have a point when she screeched at me every now and then, "Andrew, stop touching your nose!" Andrew, stop fidgeting. Andrew, stop biting your nails. And so on. All that changed when I became an accredited boxing coach. It turns out that body language is important in the ring as well, so to this day, I still practice what I call the mirror image. Particularly when conflict or challenges are anticipated in the day ahead, I check myself in the mirror to make sure that my posture is good and that I am fully in control of my circumstances.

5. Assertiveness in Social Settings

Think twice before you speak, because your words and influence will plant the seed of either success or failure in the mind of another. The key to successful leadership today is influence, not authority. -Napoleon Hill

One of the earliest lessons Henry was given as a teenager by his father turned out to be ironic. While his father encouraged him to man up and start thinking for himself as a man should, it was always hard for Henry to put this advice into practice. After all, it felt as though most of the decisions were already being made for him. His father decided what was best for him. Instead of going to university, Henry would have to learn to fend for himself and go and look for a steady job, just like every other young man his age in his working class neighborhood was doing.

Like acclaimed American author Napoleon Hill, Henry had high hopes of becoming a full-time writer. If he couldn't go to college or university to hone his literary skills, he could still bury his head in a ton of books and learn to emulate the greats, from the great Charles Dickens to Irish writer Paul Lynch. But like Hill often taught his many readers over a period of decades, Henry wanted to make money by writing about the things that interested him the most. Little did Henry realize just how competitive the writing world was.

Henry lacked the ambition to do anything about his thoughts. He was influenced by negative perceptions about his shortcomings as a young man, never mind as a writer. *"Don't you have to be clever to be a writer?"* his mother would often ask him when he ranted and raved about wanting to be a writer instead of being stuck in a dead-end sales job that he was clearly not cut out for.

Indeed, during those rare moments that Henry actually decided to do any writing, he lacked the authority that would surely influence future readers to sit up and take notice. Even so, he learned his lesson. Four months on from the promotion and having spent plenty of that time poring over self-help books, sticking to just a few basic healthy habits, physically facing his fears and reflecting on his experiences - it was beginning to pay off.

Understanding Social Interactions

No matter how much he learned from his reading of self-help books, Henry was forced to acknowledge that when it came to practicing what he had learned, he had to have the company of others. After all, talking to himself in the mirror doesn't exactly simulate a real conversation, but it's still a good way to start!

At this stage, Henry didn't feel confident enough to make small talk with people who he didn't know very well, as still he assumed that they wouldn't be interested in speaking to him. But he did have his friends. That being said, your trusted friends who don't mind your peculiar habits allow you the space to just be yourself. This is a great place to start practicing assertive communication skills.

Spending time with friends and family members, you trust in what we are going to refer to as low-stakes situations will help you to build the necessary momentum to deal with real-life situations in which other men, already accustomed to their roles as assertive providers and protectors, might take for granted. Additionally, it equips you to make informed decisions, both in personal relationships, where decisiveness is often expected, and in the workplace, where strong decision-making is essential for success.

Start With Low-Stakes Situations

Henry's friend from two doors down suggested one fine Saturday morning that he should meet her downtown for a cup of coffee. Since he had nothing better to do and he was feeling the pinch of loneliness. He thought, *"Why not?"*

Henry and Linda met at the library a few months ago. It was Linda who first introduced herself to Henry after noticing him studying history, a subject she was passionate about too. While Henry sensed that she was interested in him, he didn't feel the same way. Still, he kept things friendly; he valued her perspective and appreciated having a female friend, especially since he didn't have any.

Henry saw the coffee date role-playing exercise as a chance to prepare for real dating. After all, he'd been sticking to his new healthy habits for a while and was starting to believe that he is worthy of receiving female attention. He asked Linda if they could treat the scenario like a real date.

Although the request slightly annoyed her, since she genuinely hoped for something more, she agreed, knowing she would still enjoy the attention and wanted to help Henry out.

Just before leaving the house for the date, Henry took a moment to center himself. He stood in front of the mirror, adjusting his posture to appear more confident, shoulders back, chin up, relaxed but intentional. He quietly rehearsed how he would greet Linda with warmth and respect, reminding himself of the basics: make eye contact, smile genuinely and stay present in the conversation.

Finally, it was time. Henry felt a flicker of nervousness as he arrived at the coffee shop, but it quickly faded when he greeted Linda with a warm hug. Conversation flowed easily, mostly from Linda's side, but Henry made a genuine effort to stay engaged. He maintained steady eye contact, asked thoughtful questions, and did his best to show he was listening. The only thing missing was any real flirtation. Henry found it difficult to offer compliments or create romantic energy, largely because he didn't feel attracted to her and didn't want to send mixed signals.

The meeting was a work in progress, and baby steps had been taken.

Still, it was a step forward. Henry left the coffee shop feeling noticeably better about himself and grateful for the experience. He thanked Linda sincerely for helping him out, and when she offered feedback, he listened and took it to heart. Henry now feels motivated to use this role playing situation to help him assert himself in the office and many other areas of his life.

For any social situation you're preparing for, whether it's a date, a job interview, or joining a group discussion, you can create a low-stakes practice scenario. Politely ask a friend or family member to help you with a role-playing exercise to gain confidence and experience. That said, if you find yourself in a situation like Henry's, where your practice partner has genuine feelings for you, it's important to set clear boundaries early on. Doing so helps avoid misunderstandings or hurt feelings. Fortunately, in Henry's case, Linda agreed to remain just friends after their meeting.

Exposure Therapy

Exposure therapy is a psychological treatment that involves gradually and repeatedly facing fears or discomfort in a safe, controlled way. It's commonly used to treat anxiety disorders, phobias, PTSD, and social anxiety, but its principles can also be applied to help you become more assertive, especially if your passivity stems from fear of conflict, rejection, or judgment. Essentially, it's the practice of escalating low-stakes situations into medium- or even high-stakes ones.

The truth is, low-stakes situations can only take you so far. Their purpose is to help you practice new behaviors in a safe, low-pressure environment—but without real challenge, there's limited growth. To truly make progress, you need to gradually step outside your comfort zone and embrace situations that create a bit more discomfort. Below are some examples of how to scale up these challenges over time.

(Example 1)

Low: Asking a stranger for the time.

Medium: Ask a stranger for directions, then make small talk about the area for 1–2 minutes, such as asking recommendations for restaurants.

High: Ask a stranger for their opinion on something personal or meaningful. *"What do you think makes a great friend?" "What should you look for in a partner?" "What's your biggest goal in life?"*

(Example 2)

Low: Giving a polite opinion in a group setting.

Medium: Expressing a mild opinion in a group conversation. *"Actually, I disagree with that..."*

High: Initiate a difficult conversation with a close friend or family member about something important or sensitive.

    While you may think that it is strange to start a deep conversation with a stranger, who cares? The worst that can happen is they ignore you. This is exactly how exposure therapy is a powerful way to desensitize yourself to discomfort. The more you confront situations that trigger anxiety, the less power those situations hold over you. With repeated practice, what once felt intimidating starts to feel manageable, even routine.

Over time, consistent effort builds confidence and rewires how you respond in social situations. As you gain real-world experience, you begin to see that assertiveness often leads to respect, not rejection. That's also why many men tend to come into their own in their late twenties or early thirties: they've built up enough experience, and taken enough small risks, to break free from old fears and step into a more confident version of themselves. That being said, don't put too much pressure on yourself to sort your life out so soon, you are still young and have many years to discover who you are.

Reading the Room

If you lack the ability to read the room, you'll struggle to align with the social and emotional tone of any situation. For instance, if two people are engaged in a serious, deep conversation and you suddenly join in with high energy and humor, you won't just disrupt the flow, you'll also likely come across as disrespectful.

Adapting your message based on the mood and energy of others allows you to tailor both what you say and how you say it, making your communication more relevant and respectful. By responding thoughtfully to people's feelings and cues, you build trust and establish a stronger connection. This awareness also helps you avoid missteps, steering clear of topics, jokes, or tones that might offend or alienate others. Ultimately, showing this level of emotional intelligence helps your conversations flow smoothly and you certainly gain respect from others.

So how do you read the room? Well it all starts with you observing the conversation. If you are approaching a person or group of people to communicate with, take into account the following:

- **Observe body language and facial expressions** - Look for nonverbal cues like crossed arms (defensiveness), leaning in (engagement), or fidgeting (nervousness). This gives you a decent picture of how people are feeling in the conversation. If people are nervous, give them space and don't get too personal, if people are engaging well with you, feel free to pick up the pace of the conversation with humour or intimacy.
- **Listen to the tone and energy of conversations** - A slow, hesitant tone may signal discomfort, while a fast-paced, excited voice may show enthusiasm. Ideally you want to match the tone of the conversation.
- **Be aware of group dynamics** - Are people agreeing naturally, or is there visible tension? If a group suddenly goes quiet after someone speaks, it could indicate disagreement or discomfort.
- **Adapt based on the mood** - Every conversation is different depending on the subject, I cannot sit here and give you instructions on what to say all the time because that takes away from your personality. Just ensure you can read the atmosphere and find ways to add to it or take away from it. For example humorous

conversations should invite you to add your own jokes, whereas serious conversations require empathy and perhaps a subject change to prevent tension building.

- **Pay attention to personal space** - If you notice people are distant or closed off, don't attempt to force yourself in their proximity as they aren't interested and may be uncomfortable. This goes for speaking to women you find attractive at the bar, if they clearly show you they're not interested, respectfully leave them alone.
- **Trust your gut instinct** - If something feels off, it probably is. As you gain experience with a wide variety of conversations, you will begin to understand how people are feeling and whether your input to the conversation is invited or not.

Breaking the Ice

There is often a significant barrier that prevents potential friendships, romantic connections, or even important decisions from taking shape, and that barrier is the lack of a genuine icebreaker. Breaking the ice is the essential first step to starting meaningful conversations, easing social tension, and creating space for deeper connection, especially when meeting someone new.

Many men don't get a second date simply because they failed to move beyond surface-level small talk. Playing it too safe and avoiding authentic or engaging conversation often leaves the other person feeling uninterested or disconnected.

Breaking the ice helps overcome awkwardness, opens the door to meaningful interactions, and sets a positive tone for future conversations. Breaking the ice can feel challenging because your reserved nature makes it tempting to play it safe, but once you take that first step, it becomes much easier moving forward. You can start by asking open-ended questions, offering genuine compliments, or sharing a relatable observation about the surroundings. Great ice breakers for many situations include:

General Ice Breakers

- *"How do you know everyone here?"*
- *"What's your favorite way to spend a weekend?"*
- *"If you could travel anywhere right now, where would you go?"*

Work or Networking Events

- *"What do you enjoy most about your job?"*
- *"How did you get started in your career?"*
- *"Have you worked on any exciting projects recently?"*

Social Gatherings or Parties

- *"Where do you think is the best night out?"*
- *"What do you normally do outside of work?"*
- *"If you won a million dollars and had to spend it today, what would you spend it on?"*

First Dates

- "What's something you're passionate about that most people wouldn't guess?"
- "Let's say we're stranded on a deserted island, what three things are you bringing?"
- "What's something on your bucket list you haven't done yet?"

I'm sure you can come up with ice breakers that fit your personality far better than that generic list. If you're a bit strange, don't be afraid to ask unusual questions, as long as they're respectful and appropriate! Beyond that, having the ability to shift the mood or dynamic of a group is a powerful communication skill that others will genuinely admire. Imagine walking into a room and instantly lifting everyone's spirits. While that might seem out of reach right now, with focused effort on building your charisma, it's definitely achievable. Here are some effective ways to develop your charisma:

- Embrace your strengths and imperfections, don't take yourself so seriously, have a laugh.
- Smile sincerely, use open body language, and express enthusiasm. Positivity is contagious and draws people toward you.
- Sharing personal experiences makes you more relatable and memorable. Good storytelling can captivate and inspire. To have good stories to tell, live your life to the fullest.
- Understand and acknowledge others' feelings and perspectives. When people feel understood, they naturally gravitate toward you.
- Don't try to be someone you're not. Charisma comes from authenticity, being honest and true to yourself encourages others to do the same.
- Light humor can break down barriers and make interactions enjoyable. Just be mindful of the context and your audience.

Please remember that you cannot please everyone. If you join a group discussion or go on a date and pick up on negative nonverbal cues, don't feel pressured to win their approval, especially if it would involve changing your character. There's no shame in stepping away and finding a social setting where you feel more comfortable and accepted.

Coming Out of Your Shell

You may now be at a stage where you experience a quiet but firm sense of assertiveness within your own mind, yet when the moment arrives, whether in a conversation, confrontation, or decision-making situation, your inner assertiveness fails to materialize in action. Internally, you may know what to say and believe you have the right to say it, instead, you default to silence, avoidance, or people-pleasing behaviors.

This disconnect between inner conviction and outward behavior is frustrating. I was once there, it was like no matter how hard I tried to put myself out there and show my personality, I had a mental block that simply didn't allow for it. Here are two strategies that personally helped me come out of my shell. I started by applying them in low-stakes situations and gradually built up to more challenging ones.

One powerful tool for breaking out of habitual passivity is a technique from *Dialectical Behavior Therapy* called *Opposite Action*. The basic idea is that when your instinct tells you to shrink, withdraw, or stay silent, do the opposite. Not recklessly, but in a deliberate, mindful way. For example, if your reflex is to give a blunt answer out of nervousness, when somebody asks you an open-ended question, challenge yourself to expand your answer and even ask a similar question back to them.

Another effective technique is the use of pre-commitment strategies. These involve creating a small system of accountability that nudges you toward taking action, even when your instinct is to avoid it. For instance, if you tend to hold back in meetings or group discussions, tell a trusted friend or coworker ahead of time: *"I'm going to speak up once in this meeting."* Then ask them to check in with you afterward. Knowing that someone else is aware of your intention raises the stakes just enough to push you through the discomfort.

The goal of coming out of your shell isn't to force yourself into being someone you're not, it's to become comfortable around others as quickly as possible, because that's when your real personality begins to show. When you're at ease, you're not overthinking every word or gesture. You laugh more freely, share more honestly, and respond more naturally. It helps your relationships deepen quicker, because people can sense when you're being authentic.

Practice Makes Perfect

While the assertive habits covered in the previous chapter will develop your social skills, this section allows you to focus specifically on the areas of your communication that you want to improve for your own personal benefit. First, let's recap the basics of assertive communication. Whenever you're communicating with someone or approaching a person or group, it's important to keep the following in mind at all times:

- Use "I" statements when expressing your needs.
- Maintain eye contact, aim for 50-70% of the time.
- Speak clearly and calmly. Use a steady, even tone, avoid mumbling or shouting.
- Set boundaries. Politely but firmly state your limits and what you're comfortable with.
- Practice active listening. Show you're engaged by nodding, asking questions and summarizing what the other person says.
- Be direct and specific. Clearly state what you want or need without being vague.

- Use open body language. Stand or sit upright with relaxed shoulders and uncrossed arms.
- Say no when needed. Decline requests respectfully without feeling guilty, also avoid over apologizing.
- Ask for clarification. If something isn't clear, ask questions rather than making assumptions.

The Mirror Exercise

Now that you've been reminded of the key assertive communication skills, let's return to low-stakes situations where you can begin practicing. Start by using a mirror to rehearse on your own, and later, try role-playing scenarios with a partner, or even a small group. This is the equivalent of regular shadowboxing for boxing training. For these exercises to be truly effective, they should involve thoughtful planning and reflection. Whether you're working with a partner or practicing solo using your journal, consider asking yourself the following questions:

- *What communication skills do I want to improve?*
- *What situation do I want to recreate?*

Also, before the exercise starts, ground rules should be set. Because you are starting from a low base long before you are ready to step up to the plate, you should have low expectations about what you can achieve. It will take time and patience to achieve sought-after results, but you will reach your role-playing goals sooner than you think when you fully immerse yourself in the scenario being played, focusing on how you use your voice, body language, facial expressions, and even hand gestures.

The mirror exercise is simply role playing, on your own, typically in front of a mirror, allowing you to observe your body language, facial expressions, and gestures in real time. It's a great starting point for building self-awareness and practicing how you carry yourself in social situations. Practicing only in front of a mirror won't take you very far, because true growth happens when you're engaging with real people. You need real-time feedback and unpredictable responses to learn how to adjust, assert yourself, and respond to social cues with confidence. Some examples of scenarios you can act out in the mirror may include:

- *Job interviews.*
- *Introducing yourself to a group.*
- *A first date.*
- *Public speaking.*
- *Small talk with a stranger.*
- *A difficult conversation with somebody you care about.*

You can rehearse almost any situation using the mirror exercise, it's a great way to prepare mentally and refine how you express yourself. It's especially useful for public speaking or presentations. Although the pressure of a real audience can be intimidating, practicing your script 20–30 times in front of a mirror can build the confidence you need to deliver it smoothly.

Exercise 9 - Role-Playing Scenarios

Role-playing can pose a bit of a challenge if you are shy and reserved. It is certainly a step up from the mirror exercise, but I urge you to take the plunge and try out role-playing with someone you love and trust.

What you ultimately say or do should reflect a newly created sense of independence. You are thinking independently, and you are acting independently of others. You are your own boss. That being said, don't be afraid to discuss the things that interest you, tell people about the things you'd like to achieve in life and make your personality known to others. Below are some examples of role playing scenarios to try:

Setting a Boundary with a Friend

- **Scenario:** A friend repeatedly shows up late or borrows things without asking.
- **Goal:** Practice expressing your needs and enforcing personal boundaries.
- **What to Try:** *"Look mate, I really appreciate our friendship, but you need to stop wasting my time by*

turning up late. I have things to do, in future just let me know if you'll be late or can't make the time."

Initiating a Difficult Conversation

- **Scenario:** You feel like your partner isn't being her usual self, sparking trust issues from your side.
  Goal: Practice initiating honest emotional dialogue without shutting down or deflecting.
- **What to Try:** *"I've noticed that you seem a bit distant lately, and I just want to check in. I'm not trying to accuse or blame, I'd just really appreciate it if we could talk about how we're both feeling."*

Flirting or Expressing Romantic Interest

- **Scenario:** You want to ask someone out or compliment them genuinely.
- **Goal:** Practice expressing interest without fear of rejection or over-apologizing.
- **What to Try:** *"Hi, I just want to let you know that I like your outfit and find you very attractive. Could I get your number?*

Confronting Somebody Who Treats You Poorly

- **Scenario:** Someone in your life consistently talks down to you, ignores your boundaries, or makes you feel small. You've let it slide before, but now you've had enough.
- **Goal:** Assert your needs and self-worth by setting a clear boundary without resorting to aggression or self-blame.
- **What to Try:** *"I need to talk to you about something that's been bothering me. Each time you talk over me in a group discussion like I'm not even there, it really frustrates me. I'd appreciate it if you let me finish what I have to say."*

When doing an exercise for the first time, don't be afraid to experiment, try out new things, and even make mistakes. After all, when mistakes are made, you can only learn from them. Plus, this is the best time to mess up! While your role-playing partner can give you feedback-they can also act as your accountability coach-you can use your journal to self-reflect.

Public Speaking

Speaking publicly may sound terrifying for you. But you know what that means, with plenty of practice it brings you the most confidence, significantly improves your communication skills and develops your character to a whole new level.

So while you still need to get used to raising your voice so that others can respond to it deferentially or respectfully, let alone hear you, you still need to get over the bundle of nerves associated with first-time public addresses.

Ask any great leader from the past to the present, from Churchill to Obama and even Donald Trump, and they will always say the same thing. It's nervous in the beginning. But it gets better after practice. One of the smartest tricks that these gentlemen have learned over the years is to first get to know their audience. Relate to them in ways that bring only nods of approval rather than hoots of disagreement. Below are some tips for public speaking in no particular order.

- **Start small and safe.** Start speaking in small groups, team meetings, or even practice in front of a mirror. Progress to slightly larger groups as your confidence builds.

- **Use your strengths.** Being quiet or thoughtful isn't a weakness, use your calm presence to deliver thoughtful, clear messages.
- **Prepare thoroughly.** Preparation builds confidence. Know your topic well, plan your key points, and practice your speech out loud until you hate the sound of your own voice. Rehearsing reduces anxiety and helps you stay grounded.
- **Practice in a mirror.** This helps you observe your body language, tone, and pace. You can also spot nervous habits and improve your delivery.
- **Use notes smartly.** Don't be afraid to use cue cards or bullet points to stay on track. Just avoid reading word-for-word, it flattens your delivery and makes you seem nervous.
- **Focus on the message.** Instead of worrying about how you're being judged, shift your focus to the message you're trying to share. Remind yourself: *I'm here to offer value.*
- **Embrace the pauses.** Silence isn't always awkward, it's powerful. Use short pauses to gather your

thoughts and emphasize points. It shows control, not hesitation.

- **Expect nerves.** It's normal to feel nervous. Don't wait until you feel fearless. Courage means speaking despite the nerves, not without them.
- **Get feedback.** Ask for feedback from people you trust and use it to improve. The more you speak, the easier it gets, consistency is key.

This exercise may not align with your current needs or goals. However, if you do decide to give it a try, remember this: successful speakers engage their audience from the very beginning. They've likely spent hours practicing in front of a mirror, paying close attention to their body language, tone, and even their facial expressions. It's not just about what you say, it's about how you carry it.

Your Call to Strive for Discomfort

Going back to exposure therapy and role playing scenarios, it's time for you to up the anti and put yourself in situations your old passive self would hate. Think back to the list you made for exercise 4, you have many reasons why you want to be assertive, you probably have even spent many nights imagining yourself being assertive and reaping some kind of reward in many different scenarios, it is now time for you to put those dreams to reality. But in order to do so, it takes some initiative from yourself.

You see, as much as I'd love to know about every high and low on your journey from passive to assertive, the truth is, unless you reach out (please feel free to), I don't know who you are, what you're struggling with, or why becoming more assertive matters to you. I've done my best to make this guide as helpful and relatable as possible for a wide range of boys and men, drawing from my own experiences and the work I've done with other young men. But I know it's not perfect, there's always room to grow.

Yet again, please leave an honest review of this guide. It helps me improve it for others who might be walking a similar path.

Anyway, you need to identify the specific scenarios, situations, and fears that hold the most power over you, and work on turning that discomfort into just another day at the office. For me, as a young passive man getting started with boxing, I was most intimidated by the thought of having to coach others. The responsibility felt overwhelming, and I constantly feared being judged or not taken seriously, furthermore I didn't even feel competent enough to teach certain techniques properly.

So how did I overcome it? Honestly, I have my old boxing coaches to thank. Part of our training involved students stepping to the front of the gym to lead a technique or exercise. It was terrifying at first. The first dozen times were brutal, I could see the discomfort on the other boxers' faces, like they felt secondhand embarrassment for me. I honestly came close to quitting boxing altogether, many times. But being thrown that far outside my comfort zone forced me to confront my fears and accept my insecurities head-on. Yes, I embarrassed myself. Yes, I looked nervous and sounded unsure. I even had to have a coach step in to say what I was teaching wasn't correct. It humbled me, and at the same time, it built my confidence in ways I never expected. I have come a long way since then and I hope you can say the same thing years down the line.

You need to aim for that same level of discomfort, the kind that stretches you, not breaks you. Ideally, this should relate to the areas of life where you want to become more assertive, but honestly, I recommend pushing yourself in many areas of your life, within reason. That doesn't mean using this as an excuse to do something reckless. But experiences like skydiving, caving, or even quitting a job you hate can become turning points. These are the kinds of moments that shake you up and spark real growth. Sticking to the theme of this guide, here are a few discomfort-driven challenges you can take on to build your assertiveness from the inside out.

1. Join a conversation club.
2. Attend networking events.
3. Host small gatherings.
4. Practice storytelling or reading aloud.
5. Start a podcast or YouTube channel.
6. Join a martial arts or fitness club.
7. Try 100 days of rejection.
8. Go solo travelling for a month.
9. Start a side hustle and tell everybody about it.
10. Spend a day without your phone.
11. Do something you've always wanted to do but have been too afraid to try.

12. Volunteer to lead a meeting or present an idea.
13. Admit a mistake publicly and take responsibility.
14. Ask for help when you'd normally suffer in silence.

6. The Key to Strong Relationships

The most important ingredient we put into any relationship is not what we say or what we do, but what we are. And if our words and our actions come from superficial human relations techniques rather than from our own inner core, others will sense that duplicity. We simply won't be able to create and sustain the foundation necessary for effective interdependence. – Stephen Covey

Some of you reading this may still be in school and haven't even thought about dating or relationships yet, and that's completely fine. I didn't enter my first relationship until my early twenties, so please don't feel any pressure to rush into it. That said, now is a great time to start learning how to communicate confidently and respectfully with women. Developing these skills early will save you a lot of confusion, heartache, and awkward moments down the road.

Many of us imagine meeting someone special, maybe at a coffee shop, a concert, or just by chance. When that moment comes, you'll want to be prepared to show up as your best self and make a genuine connection. Furthermore, this chapter will also provide tips on how to build new relationships and strengthen current relationships with friends and family using assertive techniques.

It's back to pen and paper for Henry as he reflects on his pretend date with Linda. He's proud of the progress he's made, having not been on a date for years, but he knows there's still room to grow.

That said, things are improving—five months have passed since Chris won the promotion over Henry, and much has changed since then. He now prioritizes his gym sessions, going religiously 4 times a week, he has cut down on drinking, only allowing himself to have a couple of beers every Saturday, he has moved out of his mother's house into his own flat - making use of his savings and not allowing his mother to live his life for him, he's changed his style, he's been tracking his small wins of being assertive in low stake situations and social settings, and he finally appreciates the man looking back at him in the mirror. With his confidence rising, Henry decides it's time to dip his toes into the dating scene for real. He downloads a dating app, hoping for the best.

Henry doesn't expect much. Deep down, he knows that meeting a meaningful love interest probably won't happen online, it's more likely to occur out in the real world. But there's one problem: he still lacks the confidence to make the first move in person. While he's starting to get more comfortable with rejection and is slowly learning how to handle it, the idea of being turned down face-to-face still feels unbearable. That's assuming he can even get the words out in the first place.

It's never been like that for Chris, though. He's faced rejection from women countless times, whether on nights out or in everyday encounters, yet it never seems to faze him. Chris just keeps going, undeterred. And to be fair, he does have a certain charm. Though he faced many rejections, he also enjoyed plenty of successes. His bold, confident approach, driven by his aggressive (now assertive) nature, has often enabled him to work his charm.

Indeed, Chris was one of those guys who always got his way with women, but what are we missing here when I suggest to you that the bully in the room is getting his way? Does this mean that he is influential and assertive enough to impose himself on others, using the gifts of his manhood? Is it his ability to take up space and lead interactions without hesitation? Is he behaving in a way that is expected of other women who can't stop gawking at his height and finely chiseled muscles?

I'll let you into a secret. It's not rocket science, either. Yes, it is true that women value strong men, particularly those who are able to assert themselves with relative ease and without feeling guilty. Such men are comfortable with their masculinity, and asserting themselves comes naturally to them. Strength, both physical and emotional, is undeniably attractive, but it's the ease with which these men own it that makes the real difference.

Understanding Relationships

30 matches later and finally, Henry got a message back from Sophia, a beautiful young lady that he matched with online. After days of messaging back and forth, talking about shared interests and life aspirations, Sophia took up Henry's offer to go to an Italian restaurant one evening for a date. Henry, captivated by both her natural beauty and unfiltered personality, feels genuinely motivated to put his best foot forward, hoping it leads to a second date.

In the days leading up to the date, Henry did everything he could to prepare. He jotted down potential conversation topics, practiced his delivery in front of the mirror, and devoured self-help books on dating and relationships. But there was one thing he couldn't fake.

Experience.

Having only ever been in one short relationship, which lacked real romance and was more of a friendship, Henry still struggled to grasp the nuances of romantic connection. Reading a woman's mind felt impossible. As the old saying goes, *men are from Mars, women are from*

Venus. We're different. Our thoughts, our emotions, our behaviors.

This was a major obstacle for Henry when it came to breaking the ice with Sophia. The only approach he knew was to build a connection the same way he would with a friend. While that can work, it often sends the wrong message, one that suggests you're not genuinely interested or that you're unwilling to take the lead. Many women simply won't wait around for a passive man to make a move, no matter how attractive they find him. If you want to give yourself the best chance at building a meaningful, lasting romantic relationship, you need to understand women, how they think, and what they value in a connection. So, what goes into a healthy relationship?

- Trust.
- Honest and open communication.
- Respecting each other's boundaries, feelings, opinions, and autonomy.
- Supporting each other during tough times and celebrating the wins together.
- Similar or shared values and goals.
- Compromise and flexibility.

- Regular meaningful time together.
- Intimacy.

Naturally, there are a few key differences between a romantic relationship and a friendship. For example, chances are you're not looking to neck off with your best friend, or maybe you are, who knows? The point is, understanding different types of relationships starts with recognizing their unique dynamics.

A romantic relationship is typically defined by emotional and physical attraction, often involving expressions of love, desire, and commitment that go beyond friendship. These relationships usually include a sense of exclusivity, particularly in committed partnerships, and are often oriented toward building a shared future, whether that means marriage, or long-term partnership. Often, to build and keep a romantic relationship thriving, you need to keep the spark alive - attraction is everything.

In contrast, a platonic relationship, such as a friendship or relationship with a family member or work colleague, is characterized by emotional closeness and affection without any romantic attraction. These relationships are typically based on mutual respect, trust, and shared experiences, and they can be just as emotionally supportive and long-lasting as romantic ones. Physical attraction serves no place here, it is more about experiencing life with people you care about.

Building New Relationships

Begin your learning curve by accepting that you will be dealing with different personality types throughout your life. When approaching a potentially promising relationship, you are required to take a different approach towards each person. This, however, does not mean that you will be shallowly adopting a chameleon-like approach to people.

To build relationships with people, whether friendships or a potential love interest, it helps to understand who they are. You can gauge whether people are outgoing and expressive, or reserved and analytical on the first time meeting them. Understanding that introverted people have a lower social battery, they prefer deeper and meaningful conversations, and that they prefer alone time over social events can help you connect with this personality type, if that's what you prefer. Tips for building relationships with introverts include:

- Respect their need for space, don't pressure them into socializing too much.
- Engage in one-on-one conversations instead of large group settings.
- Listen actively and be patient, they may take time to open up.
- Don't mistake quietness for disinterest, they just process things internally.

Whereas extroverts get their energy from social interactions, they enjoy spontaneous activities and are very talkative. Keep in mind the following tips for building relationships with extroverted people.

- Engage in conversation and match their energy, show enthusiasm!
- Be open to spontaneous plans and group activities.
- Let them express their thoughts freely, interrupting them too much can frustrate them.
- Don't take their excitement as superficial, they thrive on external stimulation.

Yet again, don't feel as if you need to change who you are to impress a girl or fit in with a new group of people, eventually they will see right through you. Always, and I mean always, be yourself, unless you don't like who you currently are - you can develop yourself to who you want to be. If you find conversing with extroverts exhausting, remember to set boundaries and don't force yourself to keep up with them. People will not give you a hard time for setting boundaries, and if they do, they aren't particularly somebody you should want to have in your life.

Keeping the Spark Alive

Even so, no matter how strong and confident you are, no matter how effective your communication skills are, and no matter how good looking you may be, building new romantic relationships has never been easy, and it's no easier to keep the spark alive in the relationship!

Building a strong romantic relationship takes intention, effort, and emotional maturity from both partners - relationships should always be 50/50! Here are key principles and actions to help build and maintain a healthy, lasting romantic bond.

Prioritize communication. This means being open and honest about your feelings, thoughts, and needs, even when it's uncomfortable. Furthermore, make an effort to truly hear what your partner is saying, rather than just waiting for your turn to speak. It's also crucial to address any issues early rather than letting resentment build over time. For example, if you feel unappreciated, bringing it up gently and with curiosity, such as saying, *"I've been feeling a little overlooked lately, and I'd like us to talk about it,"* can lead to constructive dialogue instead of conflict.

Build trust. This means following through on your words and commitments so your partner knows they can count on you. While you don't have to share every detail of your life, most definitely avoid keeping secrets and bottling up your emotions. Trust also means giving your partner the benefit of the doubt, assuming their intentions are good unless there's clear evidence otherwise. For example, if your partner forgot to respond to your message, instead of jumping to conclusions, understand they may have been busy.

Cultivate emotional intimacy. This involves being vulnerable by sharing your fears, dreams, and insecurities with your partner, which creates a safe space for both of you to be authentic. Furthermore, show empathy by actively trying to understand your partner's emotional world, this means listening without judgment, and validating their feelings by letting them know their emotions are normal and acceptable. When your partner expresses sadness or frustration, responding with something like, *"I can see why that upsets you, and it's okay to feel that way,"* instead of offering a solution to their issue as it helps them feel supported. It's also important not to apologize for your own feelings, expressing your emotions honestly, without blame, is a crucial part of assertive communication.

Respect each other's independence. Create space for yourselves by spending time apart and doing things that interest you personally. Have hobbies, friendships and goals. Have a life! Women typically lose attraction to men who are constantly by their side, creating space is healthy for any relationship. Furthermore, try to support your partner's personal ambitions and hobbies. Finally, avoid being controlling as it undermines trust, respect, and individual freedom.

Share common goals and values. Speak openly about your future, such as whether you both want children, your career ambitions, or the kind of lifestyle you envision, as it helps ensure you're aligned on the big things that matter. Creating traditions, like celebrating anniversaries in a special way or going on regular date nights, builds shared experiences that strengthen your bond over time. And it's completely fine to not share certain goals and values, as long as you show respect towards them.

Appreciate each other. Expressing gratitude daily, even for small things like making breakfast, can make your partner feel valued. Celebrating each other by offering compliments, encouragement, and recognizing each other's efforts helps build positivity and strengthens your connection. For example, saying something like, *"I really appreciate how you handled that situation today; it means a lot to me,"* shows attentiveness and care.

Don't be desperate. This is the number one turn off in a relationship, it kills attraction in relationships because it signals neediness rather than genuine desire, and humans are wired to pick up on that difference. For example, if you say *"I'll do anything to keep you,"* it can make your partner feel overly responsible for your happiness, removing equality from the relationship. While you should tell your partner how much they mean to you, don't take it too far.

Value the relationship you have with your girlfriend or spouse, and acknowledge the old adage that says: Behind every successful man stands a successful woman.

Respecting her, and being confident enough to stand your ground as a man, builds a strong foundation for love, trust, and loyalty. It helps ensure that she'll stand by you, especially when you're under pressure. I've seen this play out in real life, not just in movies. In films, we often see the tough guy leading the charge, using both muscle and wit to protect others, think of a toned-down version of Muhammad Ali, using charm and smarts to outmaneuver opponents. But when things really get tough, it's often the woman who steps up, defending her partner, not always physically, but with words that can hit harder than fists. That doesn't mean you're incapable of handling danger, it just shows how powerful true partnership can be.

When It's Time to Let Go

Henry's date with Sophia must have gone well if Sophia suggested they went for a walk along the beach the following weekend. Henry felt as if he overprepared for the date as he didn't need to rely on his list of conversation starters he made up prior, they bonded over their desire to travel the world and they both really enjoyed reading. There wasn't really an awkward moment, at least Henry thought.

Sophia remained on Henry's mind throughout the following week, distracting him even at the office. While he had started standing up for himself in some areas of his life, he still couldn't say no to the extra tasks his coworkers often manipulated him into doing. As the workload increased, his healthy routines began to slip. Henry's stress was rising and he realized he was spending too much time texting Sophia, so he pulled back and gave her less attention, without offering any explanation.

Finally the weekend came and Henry met Sophia again, however this time around, he noticed something was off. While he was ready to express his feelings to Sophia and take things further, he felt as if now wasn't the right time, but this seriously weighed on his mind and he struggled to stay present on the date with her. He struggled to engage with her, after a while they ran out of things to talk about and the spark went out. Eventually Sophia had to address this as she was beginning to find the awkward atmosphere uncomfortable.

"Sorry, Henry, but I need a lot more, and you're not giving it to me,"

Sophia was attracted to Henry and had hoped their relationship would progress during their second meeting. However, she had no desire to take the lead. To her, it seemed as though Henry had lost interest, his texts became infrequent without explanation, and during their walk on the beach, he appeared distracted and disengaged. Though Henry had a lot on his mind, he never communicated it, leaving Sophia with the wrong impression. At times, she wished he would let go of his inhibitions and show a more raw, instinctive side.

But it was not to be. While he was upset about the news and wanted to make things right with Sophia, he knew that it was best to respectfully say goodbye and carry on with his life. Perhaps he wasn't ready yet, but still this is the most progress he's made in years. He decided that from this point on his healthy habits should always come first and he will no longer tolerate the office loudmouth's dumping extra work on his desk. Now, Henry wants nothing more than to be respected at work, by everybody.

Exercise 10 - Become a Ladies Man

Let's face it, you're afraid of women, and I get it. I was too! For me, it stemmed from a deep lack of understanding and very little real experience with women. I didn't know how to connect, how to communicate, or even how to just be myself around them.

I wasn't a ladies man.

There's also a big misconception about what it means to be a ladies' man. Too often, people assume it refers to someone who is manipulative, disrespectful, or who treats women like objects to be used and discarded. But that's not it at all.

A true ladies' man respects women. He understands them, not perfectly, but with enough emotional intelligence and empathy to connect meaningfully. He listens, communicates, and carries himself with confidence, not arrogance. He doesn't pretend or play games. He's kind, grounded, and genuine, and those are the traits that naturally attract women, not cheap tricks or shallow charm. So if you're scared, you're not alone. But you will overcome that fear, and it starts now as you become a ladies man. Below are things you can do to work towards becoming a ladies man, and actionable steps below certain points.

1. **Focus on being interesting, not just attractive.** Develop your personality, interests, and stories. Read more, explore the world, and have opinions. Women are drawn to men who have depth and direction, not just a nice smile. Although being attractive still helps, so don't neglect working on your fitness goal and appearance.
    a. You may have to dabble around many hobbies or niches to find something you enjoy, but once you do, get really good at just one thing so you can talk about it with passion. Such as creating music, photography or exploring. Make this a goal of yours now and prioritize it how you feel necessary.
2. **Work on comfort, not control.** A true ladies' man makes women feel comfortable, not pressured. Be someone women can relax around, calm, warm, and non-judgmental. Learn to listen without an agenda.

a. You can develop this composure simply by being around women more. I am sure you have female friends whether at school or at work, spend more time being around them and focus on not showing signs of nervousness.
3. **Master flirting through subtlety.** Flirting isn't about cheesy lines, it's about playful energy, eye contact, and tone. A confident smirk or a light tease done respectfully does more than trying too hard. Less is more. Let pauses, eye contact, and curiosity do the work.
    a. There's no one-size-fits-all way to flirt. Everyone's got their own style, and yours will come out naturally once you've had enough practice. The trick? Go on more dates. Real ones. The more you're out there, the quicker you'll pick up on how women respond to you, and you'll learn to match their energy. And the thing is, your crush might not always be available, or even interested at first. That's fine. Date other women, even if they're not your dream girl. You're not wasting time, you're

sharpening your skills, building confidence, and getting into a rhythm.

4. **Treat women as equals, not prizes.** If you pedestal women or try to "win" them, you're putting pressure on both sides. Learn to enjoy the dynamic as two humans connecting, not a conquest. Drop the performance. Authenticity is more magnetic than any act.

    a. Plenty of men completely change who they are just to impress a woman. Don't be that guy. Even if you're eager to build a great relationship with someone you find stunning, never let desperation show, it kills attraction fast. Instead, focus on living your own life and leveling yourself up, the same way you'd build a video game character. Work on your skills, your health, your mindset. Put yourself first.

5. **Be grounded in your masculinity.** This doesn't mean being macho, it means being emotionally stable, decisive, and self-aware. Know your values, have direction, and don't abandon yourself to please others. A calm presence and sense of purpose are deeply attractive traits.

6. **Don't be afraid of rejection.** Being liked by all women isn't the goal, being respected and remembered is. The man who can stay relaxed when things don't go his way is rare, and noticed. So, embrace it.
    a. A simple exercise you can try right now? Ask your crush out. Next time you see her, tell her exactly what you like about her, then confidently suggest a specific time and place to meet. Whether it's coffee, dinner at a nice restaurant, or a fun activity, that part's up to you. What matters is showing clear intention and delivering it with confidence.
7. **Style, hygiene, and body language matter.** You don't need to be a model, but looking put-together, smelling good, and standing tall go a long way. Speak clearly, smile often, and don't fidget. Presence often speaks louder than words.
    a. Invest in a quality fragrance that suits you, experiment with new hairstyles, and keep your hair well-maintained with regular cuts, dress in a way that feels authentic but polished; even small upgrades, like well-fitted shirts or cleaner

shoes, make a difference. Finally, practice good posture and deliberate body language. Walk with purpose, make steady eye contact, and slow down your movements.

The quickest way to do all of the above is to get out there into the dating world if you're not already. I understand that some of you may be too young to start dating. While I recommend waiting until you're at least 18 to pursue romantic relationships, you can still focus on building genuine friendships with girls and creating a life that's full of interesting experiences.

Regular dating is one of the most effective ways to gain real-world experience in understanding and connecting with women. It's not about using them or being disrespectful, it's about meeting different personalities, learning from each interaction, and growing as a person. With regular dating, you get to practice skills that can't be learned from books or videos alone: confident body language, clear and assertive communication, the ability to listen well, and expressing genuine romantic interest through thoughtful gestures. Furthermore, it forces you to face discomfort, develop thicker skin, and realize that rejection isn't the end of the world!

So, if you're old enough, start putting yourself out there in the dating world. You can begin by trying online dating apps to gain some initial experience. As your confidence grows, begin approaching women in social settings, strike up genuine conversations, and, when the moment feels right, ask for their number.

A few final notes to keep in mind: Always be respectful, and always be honest about your intentions. If you're dating someone you're not deeply interested in yet, make it clear that you're simply getting to know each other rather than giving the impression you're building a future together, when you're not. The dating world can be cruel, and dating apps in particular make it easy for people to move on quickly. Because of that, feelings and moods can change suddenly, sometimes resulting in heartbreak for the other person. That's why it's important not to take every disappointment too personally. And if you're truly seeking a genuine, lasting relationship, I strongly recommend gradually moving away from dating apps and doing it the old fashioned way.

Building Your Strong Support System

All men need a good group of men around them for support. A good group of friends that are like brothers. These connections provide emotional support, a sense of belonging, and opportunities for personal growth, needs that are just as vital for men as they are for anyone else. While society has often discouraged men from expressing vulnerability with one another, strong male friendships can break that barrier and offer a safe space to share struggles, process emotions, and feel understood without judgment.

These relationships help reduce the pressure often placed on romantic partners to meet all emotional needs. For example, having a trusted male friend to talk to during a difficult time, like a job loss or the end of a relationship, can prevent feelings of loneliness from becoming overwhelming.

To be honest, maintaining strong friendships isn't all that different from maintaining a healthy romantic relationship, just without the romantic attraction. The same principles of communication, trust, and effort still apply. So, to build and keep a strong support system, you can definitely use the tips mentioned earlier. That said, here are a few additional suggestions that apply specifically to friendships:

- **Be present and consistent**. Make time for your friends, even when life gets busy.
- **Celebrate their wins**. Be genuinely happy for their successes, big or small. Showing support without jealousy or competition strengthens your bond.
- **Show up in tough times**. Be there when they're struggling, not just when it's convenient. Loyalty and support during challenges are what solid friendships are built on.
- **Share experiences**. Do things together, go on holidays, try new activities, or just hang out. Shared memories help create deeper, lasting bonds.
- **Express gratitude**. Let your friends know you appreciate them. A sincere thank-you or compliment can go a long way in making them feel valued. This

doesn't happen enough, and no it doesn't make you gay to tell your mates you love them.

Even when you get yourself in the worst situations, if you are with your best mates, they can become some of your most cherished memories.

Exercise 11 - Show Appreciation and Vulnerability

Here's a simple but powerful exercise: tell your best mate how much they mean to you. It might feel strange, but I assure you it's not. Honest appreciation is the glue that holds friendships together. Most people go through life without hearing it, so by speaking up, you deepen your bond and remind them they matter. Don't underestimate the power of saying it out loud, it can turn a good friendship into a great one.

1. **Choose the right friend:** Pick a close friend, someone you trust and value, even if you haven't said it out loud before. Perhaps it could be multiple people or a family member.
2. **Write down what you want to say:** Before speaking, jot down a few thoughts. Keep it simple. For example: *What do you appreciate about them? A time they helped or supported you? How has their friendship impacted your life?*
3. **Reach out and say it:** Either call them or tell them in person. Example script: *"Thanks for always having my back mate, I really appreciate having you around*

and I will always do my best to help you out when you need it."

4. **Notice how it feels:** After doing this, take a moment to reflect. Was it awkward? Empowering? Relieving? Write down how you felt and what the response was, even if it was just a *"cheers mate."*

When Relationships Become Difficult

Even at the best of times, relationships can be challenging. Speaking from experience, it is even more so when you are used to passively bending to the will of others. After his heartbreak with Sophia, Henry is in a pretty bad place. Instead of sulking and going back to old ways, he asked to speak with Chris, his supervisor.

Henry opened up to Chris about how missing out on the promotion five months ago really made him want to change, but no matter how hard he tries, he keeps falling back into his own ways. He explained that he keeps taking on extra jobs as he doesn't want to disappoint people and he is struggling to build or maintain any healthy relationships.

While Henry didn't expect any real advice from Chris, he mostly just wanted to give in excuses to why he hasn't been performing well at work recently. Chris thanked Henry for his honesty, then shared a piece of advice he'd been holding onto for years.

Chris told Henry plain and simple, you need to build thicker skin. Chris explained to Henry that he has his own struggles. *"I don't always feel like getting out of bed in the morning. I still have fears about what the day may hold, and I worry about what my team thinks of me every time I push them for results."*

Henry was surprised to hear that Chris has many similar difficulties to himself as he is always able to put on a brave face and get the job done. To Henry, Chris had never seemed like the type to reflect deeply on his own actions. Yet in this single conversation, Henry realized they were both striving for assertiveness, just approaching it from opposite ends of the spectrum.

To be completely honest, some fears have stuck with Chris to this present day and I'm unsure they will ever leave. The difference is that today he looks to challenge these fears the moment they enter his mind, compared to a passive man, like Henry, who would let the fears brew in his mind, leading to no action. The point is, your fears may never disappear, but the thicker your skin gets, the easier it is to brush past them.

Resolving Conflict in Relationships

This was the first time Henry had spoken more than a handful of words to Chris since the promotion. Henry had always felt as though there was an unspoken conflict simmering between them. But as he opened up to Chris now, the tension seemed to dissolve. Chris, however, appeared blissfully unaware there had ever been any at all.

Handling conflict constructively in romantic relationships requires a foundation of respect, even in the heat of disagreement. This means consciously avoiding hurtful behaviors such as insults, name-calling, or withdrawing from communication altogether. Instead of focusing on assigning blame or winning the argument, the primary goal should be to work together toward finding solutions that satisfy both partners.

Stay calm and respectful. When you and your partner disagree about moving into your first home together, avoid yelling, name-calling, or interrupting. If the conversation gets heated, say, *"Let's take a break and talk again in 30 minutes when we're both calmer."* This pause helps prevent saying things you might regret and keeps the relationship safe from emotional harm.

Listen to understand, not just to respond. Give your partner space to express how they feel without judgment. Imagine your partner shares that they feel neglected because you've been working late frequently. Instead of immediately explaining your reasons or defending your schedule, you focus on truly hearing them out. A simple *"I understand"* can help your partner know you care about their perspective and you can work on creating time for her if possible.

Focus on the issue, and find common ground. Work together to identify the underlying issue and brainstorm solutions that meet both of your needs. When you both want different things, like one preferring quiet nights in and the other enjoying social outings, work together to find a middle ground, such as alternating weekends.

Apologize sincerely and move forward. Take responsibility for your part in the conflict. A genuine apology can go a long way toward healing, simple as *"I'm sorry for shouting earlier; I didn't mean to upset you."* Don't bring up old issues in your relationship in a new argument as that shows no progress has been made.

Conflict, when approached with care, can become an opportunity for deeper understanding and personal growth rather than a source of emotional pain.

Let's be honest: you're probably less likely to get into conflict with your friends than in a romantic relationship. This isn't to say women cause most of the issues, it's more about men sometimes struggling to understand women. That said, there will still be times when you fall out with your boys. If you're anything like me, you know that arguing over minor stuff just isn't worth it. So here are some tips to help you navigate those moments smoothly.

- **Address the issue early.** Don't let resentment build. If something is bothering you, talk about it calmly and respectfully before it escalates.
- **Choose the right time and setting.** Have the conversation privately and when both of you are calm. Avoid confronting your friend in public or when emotions are running high.

- **Keep it real.** Good pals should have nothing to hide from each other.
- **Listen with an open mind.** Give your friend space to share their side. Try to understand their perspective, even if you don't agree with it.
- **Take responsibility.** If you've made a mistake, acknowledge it and offer a sincere apology. Owning your actions can open the door to healing.
- **Work toward a solution.** Discuss what needs to change to avoid future conflict. Compromise and set boundaries if needed to support a healthier friendship.
- **Let go and move forward.** Once the issue is resolved, forgive and avoid bringing it up again. Or, you could even laugh about how stupid it was, boys will be boys.

You Need Thicker Skin

Conflict is a two way street, just like respect, and so far throughout this guide I have delivered advice on how to deal with people creating issues with you, but have you ever wondered if you are the reason that conflict begins or escalates. I don't want to say you're the problem, because I have no idea who you are and what you may or may not have done, but let's assume you haven't got thick skin, or any skin at all in fact.

Thick skin is a phrase used to describe someone's ability to handle criticism, insults, or difficult situations without getting upset, offended, or discouraged.

Having said enough about what it takes to build up those much-needed assertiveness skills to seal the deal in relationships, I'd like to spend the rest of this chapter focusing on what it takes to build the proverbial thick skin. Here's how you can do it. You can begin by staying true to yourself, always remembering that you are not in a popularity contest. Putting yourself first so that you can be well, don't worry if there are some folks within your social ambit that don't like you.

If they want to say insulting things to you sometimes, then that's on their conscience, too. More importantly, whether it's your father trying to give you good advice, your lover airing her verbal laundry, or your boss trying to give you sound advice on the joys of not putting things off for another day, try not to take what they say to you too personally. Furthermore, the more you become exposed to shade being thrown at you, the easier it will become to handle it and not allow it to affect you.

Also, the day has surely come and gone for you to run away from a potential confrontation. When you feel as though your bones are about to be racked with fear, always stop what you're doing, take a deep breath, and try to put things into perspective.

- **Control your reactions**. You can't always control what happens, but you can control how you respond. Take a moment to pause before reacting emotionally, and respond with calm confidence. Just be careful not to let that pause turn into an awkward, prolonged hesitation.
- **Stop seeking approval**. You don't need everyone to like you. Focus on self-respect instead of people-pleasing. The more you depend on external validation, the thinner your skin becomes. You are your own man, live life on your terms and become the man you want to be. The sooner you stop letting the

fear of judgment control you, the better your life will be.

- **Face discomfort**. The more you put yourself in uncomfortable or challenging situations, like public speaking, confronting personal issues, or trying new things, the more your tolerance builds. Furthermore, if somebody confronts you, don't back down and let them walk all over you, stand up for yourself.
- **Build inner confidence.** We have spoken about habits and hobbies in great detail. You should know what to do at this point and you should be doing it. If you still haven't thought of something to do, join your local gym and ask the PT for a beginner training split.
- **Embrace yourself**. Nobody is perfect—not you, not anyone else. Striving for perfection is both impossible and unrealistic. If you have insecurities, that's completely normal, everyone does. The people who truly live freely are those who accept themselves as they are and don't take life too seriously. Embrace yourself.

- **Not everything is serious, and not everything is about you.** When people joke around with you, even if there's some truth to what they're saying, they usually aren't trying to hurt your feelings. It's often just playful banter or a way to connect. Giving a little back shows you can take a joke and keeps the atmosphere light and friendly. Learn to laugh at yourself sometimes. Finally, don't always assume that people are speaking badly of you if they are having a private chat.

7. Asserting Yourself in the Workplace

To be passive is to let others decide for you. To be aggressive is to decide for others. To be assertive is to decide for yourself. And to trust that there is enough, that you are enough. – Edith Eva Eger

Yet again, keeping in mind this is a guide for teens, you probably haven't begun working a full time job as of yet. However, you still need to learn how to assert yourself in the workplace, as the harsh reality is, you will spend the majority of your life working. It doesn't have to be doom and gloom, by learning to assert yourself in the workplace you are going to feel much more confident and competent in the workplace, and it will set you up for a much more successful career.

You might be wondering, why does asserting yourself in the workplace deserve its own section? Surely, it can't be that different from being assertive in a relationship or a group setting, right?

At work, there are bosses, rules, and real consequences that you don't usually have in relationships or casual groups. At the end of the day, your income is on the line and depending on your situation, money may be something you can't give up. You need to be clear and confident but also professional and cooperative. Because of deadlines and goals, you often have to be careful and thoughtful about how you speak up.

In this final chapter, we explore why your reputation matters, not just now, but throughout your entire career. We'll discuss the importance of work, how to build a strong and respectable reputation, and practical tips to advance your career. You'll also learn how to use assertive communication to navigate challenges like resolving workplace conflicts and maintaining a professional image at all times.

Your Career and Reputation Matters

Six months on, Henry knew full well that the main reason why he didn't land the much talked about promotion was that he simply wasn't able to assert himself in the workplace, Chris even reminded Henry of this in their previous chat. Which is why, as you've seen throughout the guide, he has been on a real mission to break his passive habits, build assertive habits and most importantly, express his needs. He has made great progress doing so, but there are still times in the office when Henry loses composure and goes back to his old passive ways.

I am sure you may relate to Henry, while you have been on your journey from passive to assertive, some instances have probably made you uncomfortable causing you to behave in a passive way. That's normal. We all have slip ups in traffic, and sometimes we need them to continue our learning streak.

I never said this transformation would be a walk in the park.

Unfortunately in this competitive life, there simply isn't enough room to keep slipping up at work. Whether you are a born leader or a servile packer down at a grocery store, your career is one of the most important investments you can make in yourself. It's more than earning a paycheck, it's about creating a life filled with purpose, growth, and achievement.

The best way to invest in your career is to build a respectable reputation for yourself. It's the story people tell about you when you're not in the room, the proof of your character, your work ethic, and your integrity. A strong reputation makes you unstoppable. It's what makes future employers eager to have you on their team, and what inspires others to want to work for you.

Your reputation is decided by how well you perform on a daily basis. It takes into consideration of everything: how motivated you are, how well you communicate with others, your attitude, your technical skills and job knowledge, your reliability, your ability to remain composed under pressure, your willingness to learn, the integrity and honesty you demonstrate in your work, how you accept and act on feedback or criticism, and your overall professionalism.

While that may seem a lot to take in right now, start small. Simply always strive to do the right thing. This includes always giving your best effort at work. Once you've established this foundation, this chapter will guide you on how to build and protect a strong reputation by continually improving your performance and how to stay assertive and maintain a positive self-image without burning out or overextending yourself.

Why You Need to Work

Just as you needed a clear "why" for becoming an assertive man, you also need a compelling "why" for work. So why do you need to work? Is it to provide for yourself and your loved ones? To build the life you've always dreamed of? Or to develop skills, gain confidence, and leave a legacy?

Money is "why" we all show up to work.

To be honest with you, there is no limit to how much money you can make. After all, you do need to put food on the table. If being the breadwinner holds no appeal for you, the harsh reality of the life we have been given is that no matter what we want to do and no matter what it is we would like to acquire, we need money to do that. While the saying goes, *"more money, more problems,"* becoming financially wealthy and responsible definitely comes with its own set of benefits.

- Provides you with financial security and peace of mind, a luxury many people don't have as they struggle paycheck to paycheck.
- Allows for you to have greater freedom and choice in life, such as holidays and creating lifelong memories.
- Enables you to invest in your health and well-being, hospital trips aren't cheap.
- Offers you opportunities for personal growth and education.
- Gives you the ability to support family and help others.

- Creates a safety net for emergencies and unexpected expenses, like if your car breaks down on the way home from work.

Even so, no matter what your age is and no matter how limited you may feel you are, nothing is impossible for you. It is just a matter of you getting out of bed in the morning and getting on with it. The big question is always: *"How do I start?"* But as an assertive man, you should already be asking the next one: *"How can I make this even better?"*

Let's move on to enhancing your performance, as doing so will make your "why" you need to work much more appealing.

Enhancing Your Performance

As well as becoming an assertive man, you are going to become a high performing man, because this too has multiple benefits. After all, at the end of the day, high performers are nearly twice as productive as poor performers. Also, high performers don't necessarily get to where they want to be through sheer back-breaking work. They don't get there by bullying others out of their way, either. Rather, they identify and manage those areas of their individual performance that need improvement.

High performers seek constant improvement with regular self assessment, by seeking constructive feedback from others and additionally they track their progress. *Notice how similar that is to the habits you've been building throughout this guide?* Identifying patterns in specific areas of communication, such as conversations from work meetings, allow them to pick apart areas for improvement and also gives them confidence knowing that they have managed to express their needs respectfully on a number of occasions.

First, it's important you get the basics right. Understand that your job is important and you need to remain responsible for all of your actions inside and outside of work. Ensure you are getting enough sleep before work, eating nutritious meals to fuel your body and mind, and staying hydrated throughout the day. Ensure you show up on time, you treat others how you'd like to be treated and you always approach each task with a positive attitude. More ways to enhance your performance include:

- **Start with self-awareness:** Know your strengths, interests, and values. The clearer you are about what motivates you, the easier it is to find the right path. Write down a list of them if you haven't already.
- **Set clear, achievable goals.** Have short to long-term goals. They don't need to be perfect, but a direction gives you focus. Revisit and adjust them as you grow.
- **Build a strong work ethic.** Be dependable, punctual, and willing to go the extra mile. Early in your career, your attitude often matters more than your experience. Keep knocking on that door, eventually it will open!
- **Keep learning.** Stay curious. Take courses, read, ask questions, and learn from those ahead of you. Skill-building is a long-term investment. Take a notepad and pen out to tasks with you and note down the best way of completing the task. At the end of each day, take 5 minutes to revisit what you learned or the mistakes you made and how to avoid them next time.

- **Seek feedback and use it.** Don't fear criticism. Ask for input and apply it to improve. It shows maturity and helps you grow fast. Keep at it with your pen and paper, review yourself just how a boss would review you, ask yourself if you are actually giving your best effort and find your areas for improvement.
- **Network genuinely.** Build real relationships, not just contacts. Talk to people, be curious about their work, and help where you can. Opportunities often come through people. Make your focus to give a great first impression, as people form lasting opinions about your confidence, credibility, and character.
- **Develop soft skills.** Communication, teamwork, emotional intelligence, and problem-solving are just as important as technical skills, and often more valued.
- **Stay adaptable.** Be open to change. Careers rarely follow a straight path, and the ability to pivot or grow through challenges is a major advantage. You can lose your job at any moment, always have a backup planned.
- **Find a mentor.** A mentor can give you insight, encouragement, and hard truths when needed. Learn

from their experience so you don't repeat avoidable mistakes. Look for experienced people in your workplace or even seniors in your family.
- **Take ownership.** Own your decisions, successes, and failures. Don't wait for permission to grow, be proactive, take initiative, and act like a leader before you have the title.

Let Your Reputation Precede You

Chris knew that reputation in the workplace counted for a lot, which is why he always walked around the office like he owned the place, even before he was a supervisor. The ability to be respected, and to respect others, in turn, contributes towards improved relationships and promotes co-operation in the workplace. Your foundation of respect can be built on the following five pillars, which state that you:

1. Find common ground. When in disagreement at work with a colleague, identify shared goals and work from there rather than focusing on differences.

Finding common ground is about shifting from *"me vs. you"* to *"us vs. the problem."*

2. Seek reconciliation where there is conflict. After a falling out over a misunderstanding, always be the first person to reach out. It can be as simple as a *"Sorry, I didn't mean to come off that defensive earlier."*
3. Recognize the human being behind the voice or opinion. Don't resort to attacking people just because you hear something you don't like, instead disagree with empathy and try to understand their view.
4. Invest in the common good that everybody possesses. Be kind to people, hold the door open for others, give your seat up on the bus and positively contribute towards society.
5. Fight against apathy whenever the passive mind is tempted to give up the pursuit of that common good. Avoid giving in to your old passive habits, while it may be easier to run away from conflict, you are fully aware just how detrimental that is to yourself and others.

You might be thinking, *"All of this sounds great"*, these are values worth aiming for. But then the real question hits you: *How do I actually get there? How do I earn the respect I'm craving?* Here's how:

- When mistakes have been made, be the first to apologize, but don't apologize profusely. Saying you're sorry once in a sincere voice should be enough. Furthermore, always, and I mean always own up to your mistakes, hiding from them or lying only digs a deeper hole.
- Be brave enough to raise your voice to object to incorrect decisions, workplace discrepancies, or offenses.
- Don't be afraid to ask questions of others when things don't feel right, and always keep yourself open to new ideas that may be of help in overturning the potential for conflict. Furthermore, if you are unsure about something you've been tasked with, ask for clarification before completing the task incorrectly.
- Treat others the way they would like to be treated. You can do this effectively enough by imagining how you would like to be treated.

- Long before you can be of service to others, you still need to prioritize your own needs.

After all, if you cannot help yourself, how can you be expected to help others?

Long before you give any thought to how others perceive you, you need to have a serious heart-to-heart chat with yourself about how you're feeling about yourself. Take the time to reflect: *Does my reputation reflect who I am? Am I communicating how I should be? Am I slipping back into old bad habits? What things am I hiding from others?*

Something you could do, attempt to view your life as an outsider, for example think about how people view you when communicating, are you standing up tall, chest out with your shoulders back? Furthermore, you could pretend that somebody is watching over you all the time, then you will feel less inclined to revert back to unhealthy habits like cheating on your diet or shying away from conflict or confrontation.

Right now, assuming your career is in very early stages or hasn't begun, the most important step is to start planning your career, even if you're not entirely sure of the exact direction yet. Begin by reflecting on your motivations—are you driven primarily by financial goals, personal growth, or making an impact? Consider your interests: what subjects or industries excite you, like engineering, technology, or design? Think about the skills and knowledge you'll need along the way, will further education, certifications, or training be necessary? Consider the types of people you'll be working alongside and the expectations your managers will have of you. How will you show them respect—and how will you earn theirs in return?

Once you start earning respect from others, you've already laid a strong foundation for your professional reputation, but that's just the beginning. There's always room to build it even further. How you do this will depend on the path you want your career to take and the industries you plan to work in. But generally speaking, see these many ways to build on your golden reputation in the workplace.

1. Consistently deliver results. Meet deadlines and exceed expectations whenever possible, prioritize quality over quantity.
2. Communicate effectively and maintain relationships with coworkers. Stay informed. Keep colleagues and

managers informed about progress, obstacles, and successes. Support others and give credit where it's due, team players are highly valued.
3. Demonstrate integrity. Be honest, transparent, and accountable for your actions.
4. Be solution-oriented. Focus on solutions, not just problems. If you can spot issues early and offer solutions proactively, you'll be seen as reliable and strategic, not just reactive.
5. Maintain composure in high-pressure moments. How you act when things go wrong shapes your reputation more than how you act when they're going right. Calm under fire is magnetic.
6. Develop expertise. You are responsible for knowing your job inside out.
7. Maintain a positive attitude. People will want to work with you if you energize teams rather than drain them.
8. Master perceived ownership of projects. Act as though the success or failure of a project is personally tied to you, even if you're not the lead. People notice when you take responsibility beyond your formal role.

9. Build reputation capital before you need it. Help colleagues, share credit, and offer solutions before you ever need a favor or support.
10. Craft a signature professional brand. Be known for one or two standout traits—such as always delivering ahead of deadlines, keeping meetings concise, or simplifying complex tasks.
11. Protect your credibility at all costs. Never overpromise, and if you can't deliver, communicate early. One broken promise can undo months of hard work.
12. Build cross-department alliances. Don't limit your reputation to your immediate team—cultivate relationships across the organization so your name carries weight everywhere.
13. Be the person who raises the bar. Consistently improve processes, bring new ideas, and make work easier for others. People will see you not just as competent, but as a force for positive change.

Motivations for Advancing Your Career

Why not? Why not go further than you have ever been before? If you are just starting out, it is still early days, but the more you put off pursuing the career of your dreams, the less time you will have to follow through on those dreams. The older you get, the quicker time flies, but even if you fall within that age bracket that says you are close to the official retirement age in your area, it is still not too late. In the context of this book's theme, going from passive to assertive, we could point the finger of blame at our inherent fears of not wanting to explore opportunities that may have always been there. We were too afraid to ask the right questions, like:

What do I really want to do with my life?
With just a basic education, how do I get into varsity or college?
What career would suit me best?
How much money can I make?

Seriously, write those questions down and answer them honestly.

Handling Adversity

Every adversity, every failure, every heartache carries with it the seed of an equal or greater benefit. –Napoleon Hill

Over the past few months, Henry has been steadily asserting himself in the workplace. He started small, joining lunchtime conversations with coworkers, and has since progressed to confidently and politely declining extra tasks from colleagues who once manipulated him into doing their work. Now, Henry is taking things a step further by actively seeking advice and feedback from his supervisors on how he can develop into a great leader one day.

While Henry's progress is undeniable and he's feeling more confident in himself, some days still bring adversity, and he occasionally slips back into old, passive habits. For example, after preparing diligently to deliver a presentation to his coworkers, Henry felt the intense pressure of so many eyes on him. His mind went blank, and he ended up reading off his cue cards as if he had no grasp of the subject, missing several crucial points. At the time, it seemed like a failure, but that night Henry reflected on the experience. He resolved to improve his public speaking skills and took it a step further by committing to practice assertiveness in future presentations.

Adversity is any difficult or challenging situation that tests your resilience, patience, and problem-solving skills. It can come in many forms, setbacks at work, financial struggles, health issues, personal loss, conflicts with others, or even broader societal challenges.

What makes adversity at work more challenging is that it often carries deeper consequences, largely because you spend most of your time around the same people in the same environment. For someone like Henry, who still has passive tendencies, moments of discomfort can be hard to shake off. He tends to hide away when things go wrong. And while he knows that if he responded to adversity more constructively, he could actually benefit from it, he still struggles to maintain the thick skin required to handle adversity.

It is now time you start to develop thicker skin. Because, as sure as anything, you are probably going to need it at work. No matter where you are ranked on the proverbial food chain, it is pretty tough out there. To maintain thick skin in the workplace, make a habit of the following.

Understand it's never personal. So when someone in authority reprimands you for not stepping up to the plate, take his advice like a man, assuming he has already offered you constructive advice on how to correct your behavior. Furthermore, show them that you are actively listening, take notes of their criticism if it helps. Or even if it's just a coworker giving you grief, don't reel into their bait, most likely they're looking for a reaction - you can always give some back!

Break problems into manageable steps. Large challenges can feel overwhelming, leaving you unsure where to start or how to make progress. Start by identifying the key components of the challenge, then prioritize them based on urgency and impact.

Turn frustration into something productive. Instead of stewing at your desk or letting stress build up, take a purposeful break. Physical activity, like going a few rounds in boxing, not only helps release tension but also improves your overall health, sharpens focus, and builds mental toughness. Creative activities like journaling, sketching, or tackling a small personal project can be equally effective at redirecting negative energy.

Take regular breaks if possible. Switch your mind off from the pressures of work and do something that pleases you, just as long as it is healthy and helps you to relax. Try the pomodoro technique, this entails 25 minutes of work without distraction followed by a 5 minute rest, after 4 sets of that take a longer break. This also helps boost productivity.

Bad days happen. Get over it, your life cannot only be full of sunshine and rainbows. The key is not to dwell on setbacks or let them define your mood. Instead, acknowledge the difficulty, learn from it, and move forward. Tough times are opportunities to build resilience, patience, and character. Learn to appreciate your daily challenges.

These are just a few ways to handle adversity, but it's important to remember that adversity comes in many forms and can strike at any time. Your ability to manage tough situations improves with experience, as each challenge teaches you how to respond more effectively. Some challenges, however, are too complex to handle alone. In these moments, it's not only practical but necessary to reach out for support. There is no shame in asking for help when you need it. At the same time, it's important to avoid relying on others too frequently, you still need to be your own man.

Believe me, it is not as simple as snapping your fingers and saying, *"There you go. Today, I have thick skin"* It may come in dribs and drabs, it may even come via a moment of epiphany that you wished had come at an earlier stage of your life. The thing about overcoming adversity is that it is never overcome overnight, for lack of a better way of expressing this harsh reality. But the fact remains that it can be overcome, even if it feels as though it's taking a lifetime for you to overcome your difficulties.

Conflict Resolution in the Workplace

Whether you like it or not, you need to have at least an amicable relationship with your boss. Do what you are instructed to do, by all means, and always within reason, but be brave enough to speak up when you are in disagreement or need to be objective. Resolving conflict in the workplace still demands assertiveness, so refer back to the behaviors, tips, and habits of assertive communication outlined throughout this guide. However, because there is often more at stake in a professional setting, it's important to keep the following considerations in mind.

When under pressure, immediately express your emotions. In a fast-paced workplace, you may not always have the luxury of being able to carefully plan your words or consider every angle of a conflict. Push yourself to share what's on your mind right away, even if it doesn't come out perfectly at first. The key is to build the habit of responding promptly when it matters most, so the conflict is dealt with sooner rather than later. Over time you can reflect on your action and build on this skill to remain assertive when under pressure.

Seek win-win solutions. This means standing your ground without stepping on anyone's toes. By addressing both sides' needs, you prevent conflict from escalating and build mutual respect. For example, if two supervisors both need an afternoon off, they could discuss their priorities openly, decide together which need is more pressing, and arrange for the other to take their time off on a different day.

Never back down from confrontation. If you back down easily, people will hold that against you, and some will even use it to their advantage. Staying silent often means your concerns go unheard, your workload or treatment becomes unfair, and others assume you're fine when you're not. Over time, those who notice your reluctance to speak up may push boundaries or offload responsibilities onto you, knowing you won't object.

Deal with workplace bullies appropriately. Whenever it's safe, stand up to them directly and calmly making it clear that their behavior is unacceptable and you've had enough. If the problem persists, or if you feel unsafe addressing it alone, report the behavior to your supervisor or manager, providing clear and specific examples. While no one likes to be seen as a *"snitch,"* allowing bullying to continue only makes your work life harder than it needs to be. That being said, don't bully others to get your own back, you should know better by now.

Asserting Yourself to Maintain Professionalism

It had been a month since Henry's chat with Chris, now Henry finds himself clocking in less hours at the office while still meeting the results expected of him by supervisors, he has also spent a lot more time working alongside Chris, learning the ins and outs of a supervisor's role and absorbing as much advice as he could.

What has changed?

He now says no to all demands of others asking him to finish up their work. He no longer avoids conflict, and while he doesn't put up a huge fight with coworkers who have issues with him, he certainly doesn't back down. He has learned to show respect through active listening, and he makes an effort to join group discussions when he feels he can contribute positively.

The bottom line is, Henry finally feels confident enough to assert himself at work. He has achieved the main goal he set himself six months ago, not bad! While Henry still has plenty of work to do to maintain this assertiveness under all kinds of pressure and in other areas of his life, his transformation shows that you can do it too if you dig deep and never give up.

What Henry values most now is the extra time he has gained by no longer doing other people's work. With this newfound freedom, he has pursued a lifelong passion: writing. He has started posting regular articles on topics that interest him, built a small but growing mailing list, and launched his own website. Free from the constant worry about what others think, Henry is truly beginning to enjoy his life. After months of making rigorous changes, often accompanied by great difficulty and upset, he has reached a point where he can take his life in any direction he chooses, all thanks to developing a healthy level of assertiveness.

But you could take it even further in the workplace with a high level of assertiveness. When you maintain great professionalism, others are more likely to value your contributions, rely on your judgment, and see you as dependable. This is what you need for career progression, whether you are working your way up through a company for better income or starting your own business, you need a reputation that reflects your integrity, competence, and reliability. A strong professional image reassures colleagues, clients, and stakeholders that you can be trusted to deliver quality results and handle challenges with composure. Keep in mind the following.

Work on your leadership skills. At some point in life, you'll find yourself in a leadership role, whether it's managing a team at work, running a community project, or even organizing a small group effort. Begin taking initiative by volunteering for projects that require coordination, decision-making, or creative problem-solving, and pay attention to how experienced leaders navigate challenges. Practice delegating—trusting others to own their responsibilities while offering guidance and support when needed. And never stop learning. Read books, take courses, and embrace real-world experiences.

Always keep a clear head. When something important comes to mind, whether it's a concern, an idea, or a boundary being crossed, express it promptly rather than letting it fester. Speaking up in the moment prevents misunderstandings and stops small issues from growing into larger conflicts. You could also try writing it down, the point is to get it off your mind so you can focus on the task at hand.

Be the one to do everything first. Be the first to speak in meetings, put your hand up first when asked for volunteers and be the first to offer to mentor new people at work. Show your keen interest in contributing by offering ideas, asking thoughtful questions, and stepping forward when challenges arise. In today's competitive world, you need to stand out if you want success, so take initiative and start doing the additional tasks that show others you are hungry for more responsibility.

Coping Mechanisms

As you try new things, deliberately put yourself in uncomfortable situations, and even allow yourself to make a fool of yourself, you're almost guaranteed to experience a fair share of negative emotions. It's part of the growth process.

It is often these moments that make or break you, but to stay on the right side of the fence, it is important to make use of coping mechanisms because they act as the mental and emotional "shock absorbers" that help you handle stress without being completely derailed by it. Below are a few you can try in the moment when the pressure gets too much.

Take a short break from the high pressure environment. When emotions run high you're more likely to say or do something you'll regret, make poor judgments, or misinterpret what's happening. By taking yourself away briefly and coming back with a clear mind, it doesn't mean you're avoiding the problem. It means you're creating space for your nervous system to settle.

Silently say to yourself: *"I'm feeling [anger/anxiety/frustration] right now."* Naming an emotion creates distance from it. Once you've named the emotion, you have more freedom to decide how to act, rather than letting the emotion decide for you.

Splash cold water on your face or hold an ice cube for 30 seconds. Sudden temperature change pulls your mind out of spirals. The point is to physically do something to take your mind off the discomfort.

Of course, your habits come into play as coping mechanisms also. Incorporate mindfulness practices, such as meditation or box breathing, for just five minutes a day to center your mind and regulate your emotions. Furthermore, keep in mind habits of regular exercise, healthy eating, sleep and other basic self care activities. When your body and mind are well-nourished, you have a stronger baseline for managing challenges, making it easier to respond with clarity and composure when life throws curveballs.

Do not despair when you are faced with the temptation to give up. Do not beat yourself up when you find yourself lapsing back into old habits of passivity. It is a human setback, and it happens to the best of us. But a far more enduring quality of our human nature is the ability to be resilient and bounce back from adversity. Don't put too much pressure on yourself

Keep in mind that you are the only one who can reverse the way you feel about yourself. In my case, it is usually through a few deep breathing exercises during a short walk at a steady clip that gets me right as rain, but for others, there is nothing that a short, quiet, and peaceful meditation session cannot put right. While I currently have this calm approach to handling negative emotions, sometimes in the past I've just had to work harder. Spending 20 minutes longer at the gym or staying awake for an extra hour researching psychology are ways I've turned negativity into productivity. It is down to you to discover what works for you to stay assertive and maintain professionalism.

Exercise 12 - Let Life Challenge You

Do yourself a favor, go out there, and practice your newly honed skills of assertiveness. I am not suggesting that you readily go out there to make trouble with someone who would usually like to have his way with you. I'd just like you to get a taste of what everyday life could be like for you as a man who asserts himself in the public eye. If Henry is now able to say no to requests of additional tasks at work without feelings of guilt, then so can you.

You are not being stubborn; you have your values, and as an employee, you have every right to make quiet but firm requests. You also have every right to complain if your superiors step out of line. Keep yourself resilient because no matter who or what you are dealing with, life will always challenge you.

Furthermore, you should always be looking for ways to challenge yourself. Look for new ways to step out of your comfort zone, while we have covered this point many times throughout this guide, be the first person in the room to introduce yourself, book a spontaneous solo trip to an exciting place and stop being so predictable.

Conclusion

The long and winding road that leads to your door will never disappear. I've seen that road before, it always leads me here, leads me to your door. –Paul McCartney

Seven months after the last promotion, George, the office manager, announced that another supervisor position would be opening at the start of next month. Recognizing the progress Henry had made since the previous role was filled, George approached him directly. He praised Henry's development and encouraged him to put his name forward, expressing confidence that Henry was finally ready to take on greater responsibility.

But to George's surprise, Henry doesn't put his name forward. He explains that he isn't interested, as he would much rather focus on the writing he has been pursuing on the side. Henry believes that taking on the role he once dreamed of would only take away from his valuable writing time. In addition, he no longer finds sales fulfilling and feels ready to dedicate himself to something he truly enjoys. Henry demonstrated his new assertive attitude further by expressing his intention to hand in his resignation in three months' time, eager to set out on a new path in his career.

We can all agree that Henry has made a sensational turnaround when it comes to how he communicates. Beginning this guide, you were introduced to a passive man who was controlled by fear and irrational internal beliefs. Henry lacked many things, respect from others at work, a dating life, strong relationships, healthy habits and overall, he didn't have much joy in life.

Chapter by chapter you can see the progress Henry made as he went on a journey to finally address his passive nature, which was fueled by missing out on the promotion his mother encouraged him to put his name toward. Although the story focuses on only a brief period of Henry's life, it reveals the roots of his passive habits, the ways they manifested in his daily behavior, and the influence of his upbringing. Along the way, we see the changes he implements, the mistakes he makes and learns from, his emotional responses to progress, and, ultimately, the emergence of his more assertive self after months of practice and self-reflection.

You can, and will, get there too. Henry's story serves as powerful evidence that anyone can grow from being shy and passive into becoming confident and assertive. You may find it easier than Henry did to assert yourself in relationships, or perhaps your biggest challenge will be maintaining the healthy habits discussed in Chapter 4. For some, it may take only a few months to feel assertive; for others, it may take years to fully develop lasting habits. Everybody is different. Use Henry's story, and examples from my life, as guidance to learn from our mistakes, rather than expecting identical results within the same timeframe. What matters most is that the sooner you begin addressing your passive tendencies, the sooner you can start having your needs met—ultimately leading to a more fulfilling quality of life.

Henry's life has transformed dramatically. On the day of the promotion, he felt as though he had hit rock bottom, but since then, he has built healthy habits, begun pursuing his dream of becoming a writer, and has also made remarkable progress in his dating life, making up for lost time. Furthermore, we have seen Chris square away his aggressive habits, annoyingly, he managed to do so rather quickly. Through the simple yet powerful practice of journaling, he gained control over his temper and began responding more assertively in the workplace. As a result, he was able to rebuild his reputation and earn renewed respect from those around him.

There are still moments when both Chris and Henry slip back into old habits. They have their bad days, when getting out of bed feels like a challenge, and they still make mistakes from time to time. What sets them apart, however, is that they never give up. They understand the consequences of quitting and remain committed to giving nothing less than their best effort. So now the choice is yours:

Will you continue to struggle with the consequences of remaining passive, or will you take on the challenges that come with developing yourself into a more assertive man?

Test Yourself Everyday

A quick exercise to end this guide, without judging yourself, answer the following questions. At the end of each question, you will decide whether you strongly disagree, are neutral, or strongly agree with the following statements :

- Most people know that I am more assertive than I was previously.
- If a sales clerk charges me an incorrect price, I usually let it go.
- If someone asks me to do something I haven't got time to do, I'm more comfortable now than previously saying no.
- People are still taking advantage of me.
- If someone does something that upsets me, I will talk to them about it privately.
- If I meet someone I like, I will ask her out on a date.
- Unlike in the past, I am not afraid to talk about my feelings.
- I try not to hurt other people's feelings, even if it means keeping quiet about how I've been hurt.
- I will ask a question, even if it sounds stupid.

- Arguing with others still upsets me a lot, even when I believe that I'm still right.
- If someone I know shares a strong opinion that I strongly disagree with as well, I will share my point of view with them.
- I get uncomfortable when someone disagrees with me.
- I enjoy taking part in debates.

For the time being, I think I've provided you with more than enough statements for you to think about in the weeks to come. Answer each statement as honestly as you can, and whether you side with being passive, assertive, or even aggressive, think seriously about what may have kept you in that state or what brought about the change, whether it's been positive or negative for your well-being.

You won't feel the same way about yourself every day. While moods change in relation to the circumstances of the day, you also have your strong or weak days. Dipping into a passive mood could just mean that you've had a rather tiring day and you just want to be left alone in peace and quiet for a while. You might be feeling aggressively uppity after winning a few rounds on the golfing greens, but not necessarily bullyingly aggressive with the chaps you're playing with after you jokily demand that they buy you a round down at the pub afterward.

Positive progress takes a while to develop. Don't be dismayed when you dip into days of docile despair. Give yourself a few hours to recover and get back on your feet, doing all or most of the things I have been suggesting for you throughout *Passive to Assertive*. On those days when you are feeling on top of the world, enjoy every moment while it lasts.

Being assertive doesn't only mean that you're going to be on top of your game and not let others get their way with you. It also means helping those who look as though they cannot help themselves. Being assertive gives you the ability to help those in need, not just yourself. I enjoy the sensation it gives me when I see that others are a little better because of me. You will too, of that I am sure.

Key Points and Habits

There is a lot to take away from this guide, so I've created a comprehensive list of key points and habits from each chapter. Use it as a reference as you continue your own journey from passive to assertive, I trust it will serve you well.

Life Won't Wait for You

1. Write down your passive behaviors and what situations cause them.
2. Write down when you've shown passive-aggressive behaviors from bottling up your emotions.
3. Write down which of your passive behaviors are habits, tie them next to an irrational belief you may have and regularly set yourself tasks to act against the irrational belief (REBT).

Why Become Assertive?

1. Write down a large list of reasons why you want to be assertive and keep the list visible.
2. Pick one assertive behavior discussed in this chapter to build a habit of and practice it at any opportunity.

Overcoming Obstacles to Assertiveness

1. Develop a growth mindset:
    a. Recognize fixed mindset triggers.
    b. Use "Yet" language.
    c. Embrace challenges.
    d. Learn from criticism and failure.
2. Face your current biggest fear:
    a. Identify your fear and its cause.
    b. Make a list of certain actions that link to your fear and prioritize them in difficulty, then complete each action one step at a time. (take action)
    c. Regularly face those fears and reflect as soon as you can after taking action. (reflect)
3. Challenge your negative beliefs:
    a. Identify your negative beliefs.
    b. Notice when a negative belief is active.
    c. Identify the source.
    d. Look for evidence against the belief.
    e. Reframe the thought.
    f. Act against the belief.
    g. Regular self-reflection.

4. Reprogram your habit loop: (Build Habit/Break Habit)
    a. Cue: Make it obvious/Make it invisible.
    b. Craving: Make it attractive/Make it unattractive.
    c. Response: Make it easy/Make it difficult.
    d. Reward: Make it satisfying/Make it unsatisfying.

The Importance of Habits

1. Morning journal practice:
    a. Write 1–2 sentences about your current emotional state.
    b. Write your top 3 priorities for today, things you want to accomplish.
    c. Write one thing you're grateful for.
    d. Write one thing you'll do for yourself today. Self-care or something joyful.
2. Habits to begin with:
    a. Regular exercise
    b. Limit sitting and screen time, or introduce regular breaks.
    c. Hydration and healthy eating.

d. 7-9 hours of sleep each night.
   e. Shower, brush teeth, floss and wash hands frequently.
   f. Prioritize tasks and create to-do lists.
   g. Regular reading.
   h. Regular reflection.
   i. Regular meditation.
   j. Regular visualization
3. Ways to improve your self-esteem:
   a. Surround yourself with positive people.
   b. Do the things that bring you joy.
   c. Practice self-compassion.
   d. Set achievable goals and work towards them.
   e. Focus on your strengths.
   f. Avoid comparisons.
   g. Limit distractions.
4. Understand your needs:
   a. Brainstorm your needs.
   b. Write the outcome of getting each need met.
   c. Prioritize your needs.
   d. Regularly reflect.
5. Create boundaries: *When [this happens], I will [action]*

6. Basics of assertive communication (expressing your needs):
    a. Be clear and direct.
    b. Use "I" statements.
    c. Stay calm and grounded.
    d. Anticipate pushback.
    e. Say no without guilt.
    f. Validate yourself first.
    g. Be honest, not harsh.

Assertiveness in Social Settings

1. Begin practicing in low stake situations: Role play dates, job interviews and so on.
2. Exposure therapy: Gradually step outside your comfort zone and reflect on it. Embrace new social situations such as speaking to strangers, joining group discussions, risking rejection and public speaking.
3. Reading the room:
    a. Watch body language and expressions.
    b. Match tone and energy.
    c. Notice group dynamics.

    d. Adapt to the mood.
    e. Respect personal space.
    f. Trust your instincts.
4. Breaking the ice and building charisma:
    a. Write down a list of icebreakers to use at certain social situations.
    b. Embrace your strengths and imperfections.
    c. Smile and show genuine enthusiasm.
    d. Share personal stories to connect.
    e. Acknowledge and understand others' feelings.
    f. Be authentic and true to yourself.
    g. Use light, mindful humor.
5. Opposite action - when your instinct tells you to shrink, withdraw, or stay silent, do the opposite.
6. Accountability check - Make someone else aware of your intention to raise the stakes just enough to push you through the discomfort.
7. Mirror exercise - role playing, on your own, typically in front of a mirror, allowing you to observe your body language, facial expressions, and gestures in real time.
8. Role playing situations - Practice asserting yourself in situations where you'd normally struggle. Start by role-playing with a friend or family member, and

gradually work your way up to more challenging or uncomfortable scenarios.

The Key to Strong Relationships

1. Become comfortable with masculinity and who you are.
2. Keeping the spark alive:
    a. Build trust.
    b. Cultivate emotional intimacy.
    c. Respect independence.
    d. Share goals and values.
    e. Appreciate each other.
    f. Don't be desperate.
3. Become a ladies man:
    a. Focus on being interesting, not just attractive (pursue and master a passion)
    b. Work on comfort, not control (spend more time around women)
    c. Master flirting through subtlety (practice through real dates)
    d. Treat women as equals, not prizes.
    e. Be grounded in masculinity.

f. Embrace rejection.
  g. Style, hygiene, and body language matter.
  h. Action: If you're old enough, begin dating and gain experience.
4. Appreciate your mates:
  a. Be present – Make time, even when busy.
  b. Celebrate wins – Cheer them on, big or small.
  c. Show up – Be there in tough times.
  d. Share experiences – Build memories together.
  e. Express gratitude – Appreciate and acknowledge them.
  f. Don't be afraid to be vulnerable.
5. Resolving romantic conflict:
  a. Stay calm and respectful.
  b. Listen to understand.
  c. Focus on the issue and find common ground.
  d. Apologize sincerely and move forward.
6. Resolving conflict between friends:
  a. Address the issue early.
  b. Choose the right time and setting.
  c. Keep it real.
  d. Listen with an open mind.
  e. Take responsibility.

      f. Work toward a solution.

      g. Let go and move forward.

7. Building thicker skin:
    a. Control your reactions.
    b. Stop seeking approval.
    c. Face discomfort.
    d. Build inner confidence.
    e. Embrace who you are.
    f. Not everything is serious and not everything is about you.

Asserting Yourself in the Workplace

1. Enhancing your performance
    a. Start with self-awareness.
    b. Set clear, achievable workplace goals.
    c. Build a strong work ethic.
    d. Keep learning.
    e. Seek feedback and use it.
    f. Network genuinely.
    g. Develop soft skills.
    h. Stay adaptable.
    i. Find a mentor.

  j. Take ownership.
2. Building a strong reputation:
    a. Find common ground.
    b. Seek reconciliation.
    c. Recognize the human being behind the voice or opinion.
    d. Invest in the common good.
    e. Fight against apathy.
    f. Be the first to apologize.
    g. Own up to your mistakes.
    h. Be brave enough to object.
    i. Don't be afraid to ask questions.
    j. Treat others the way they would like to be treated.
    k. Prioritize your own needs when possible.
    l. Consistently deliver results and exceed expectations.
    m. Communicate effectively and maintain relationships.
    n. Demonstrate integrity and accountability.
    o. Be solution-oriented.
    p. Maintain composure under pressure.
    q. Develop expertise in your role.

  r. Maintain a positive attitude.
  s. Take ownership of projects.
  t. Help others before asking for help.
  u. Protect your credibility.
  v. Build cross-department alliances.
  w. Raise the bar by improving processes and bringing new ideas.
3. Building even thicker skin:
  a. Don't take criticism personally; listen actively and learn from it.
  b. Break large problems into manageable, prioritized steps.
  c. Channel frustration into productive activities (exercise, creative tasks, projects)
  d. Take regular breaks to relax and recharge (e.g., Pomodoro technique)
  e. Accept that bad days happen; learn from setbacks and build resilience.
4. Managing workplace conflict:
  a. Respond quickly under pressure. Address conflicts promptly to prevent escalation.
  b. Aim for win-win outcomes. Balance your needs with others' to maintain respect.

    c. Stand your ground. Don't stay silent; assert yourself to avoid being taken advantage of.

    d. Address bullying properly. Confront safely or report; never retaliate aggressively.

5. Asserting yourself to remain professional:

    a. Develop leadership skills. Volunteer for projects, practice decision-making, delegation, and problem-solving. Learn from experienced leaders and keep learning through books, courses, and real-world experience.

    b. Maintain a clear head. Address concerns, ideas, or crossed boundaries promptly to prevent small issues from escalating. Writing things down can help.

    c. Take initiative. Be the first to speak, volunteer, or mentor; actively contribute to stand out and show readiness for responsibility.

6. Coping mechanisms:

    a. Stick to healthy habits previously discussed to be in better control of your emotions.

    b. Take a short break from a high pressure situation and come back with a clear mind.

    c. Name your emotion in your head to prevent it from taking control of you.
7. Let life challenge you, get out there and give all of life's challenges your best effort.

Final Message

There's nothing more important than going after what you want, even if it's just taking the first step to try. You can seriously achieve anything you put your mind to. Life always works out for those who never give up.

Life is the most beautiful thing. What's best about it is that you are in complete control of what you do, who you choose to spend time with and the memories you create. Generations upon generations lived, loved, and fought through their own storms so that you could stand here today. Get out there and enjoy your life while you can, don't miss out on living your life, trust me you'll regret it.

Thank you for taking the time to read this guide, I would greatly appreciate it if you could leave an honest review of this guide, it helps me make improvements for a broader audience.

Andrew Hudson

References

Ackerman, C. (2019, May 27). *49 communication activities, exercises & games.* Positive Psychology. https://positivepsychology.com/communication-games-and-activities/

Allen, T. (2023, April 1). *7 things you absolutely must do if you want to be respected.* Forbes. https://www.forbes.com/sites/terinaallen/2019/10/04/7-things-you-absolutely-must-do-if-you-want-to-be-respected/

Arocho, J. (2021, April 12). *Assertive vs. agressive: what's the difference?* Manhattan Center for CBT. https://manhattancbt.com/assertive-vs-aggressive/#:~:text=Assertive%20communication%20shows%20respect%20for,someone%20without%20listening%20to%20them.

Arzón, R. (2023, February 22). *Self-respect: 5 ways to respect yourself.* MasterClass. https://www.masterclass.com/articles/self-respect

Assertiveness test. (n.d). Psychology Today. https://www.psychologytoday.com/za/tests/personality/assertiveness-test

Brooten-Brooks, M. (2024, July 16). *How to set healthy boundaires with anyone.* verywellhealth.

https://www.verywellhealth.com/setting-boundaries-5208802#:~:text=The%20key%20is%20to%20start,is%20more%20with%20boundary%20setting.

Cassata, C. (2023, June 5). *Assertiveness can improve your relationships—here's how.* Verywellmind. https://www.verywellmind.com/assertiveness-can-improve-your-relationships-7500841

Cherry, K. (2023, July 27). *Albert Ellis biography.* Verywellmind. https://www.verywellmind.com/albert-ellis-biography-2795493

Cocivera, T. (2018, May 29). If your reputation truly precedes you, what does it say?. *Forbes.* https://www.forbes.com/sites/forbescoachescouncil/2018/05/29/if-your-reputation-truly-precedes-you-what-does-it-say/

Drummey, K. (2022, October 13). *What is rational emotive behavior therapy?.* WebMD. https://www.webmd.com/mental-health/what-is-rational-emotive-behavior-therapy

Emamzadeh, A. (2024, November 8). 3 science-based tips on how to break bad habits. *Psychology Today.* https://www.psychologytoday.com/za/blog/finding-a-new-home/202410/3-science-based-tips-on-how-to-break-bad-habits

Facing adversity at work? 10 ways to build a thicker skin. *YEC*. https://www.forbes.com/councils/yec/2020/05/19/facing-adversity-at-work-10-ways-to-build-a-thicker-skin/

Field, B. (2024, May 14). *7 surprising ways to make your relationship even better.* Verywellmind. https://www.verywellmind.com/7-surprising-ways-to-make-your-relationship-better-5094212

5 1/2 things about growth mindset from Dr. Tromp. (2021, September 13). Boise State University. https://www.boisestate.edu/student-life/5-1-2-things-about-growth-mindset-from-dr-tromp/

5 rules for setting SMART goals. (n.d). *Human Kinetics.* https://us.humankinetics.com/blogs/excerpt/5-rules-for-setting-smart-goals

Foroux, D. (2016, April 18). *5 ways to build a thick skin so you can live happily.* https://dariusforoux.com/thick-skin/

Gupta, S. (2024, July 19). *How does exposure therapy work?.* Verywellmind. https://www.verywellmind.com/exposure-therapy-definition-techniques-and-efficacy-5190514

Herrity, J. (2023, July 31). *4 types of communication styles and how to improve yours.* Indeed. https://www.indeed.com/career-advice/career-development/communication-styles

How can you build effective relationships with people of different personality types?. (2023, October 24). LinkedIn. https://www.linkedin.com/advice/0/how-can-you-build-effective-relationships-soebf

How can you practice communication skills with role-playing?. (2023, August 16). LinkedIn. https://www.linkedin.com/advice/1/how-can-you-practice-communication-skills-role-playing#:~:text=By%20role%2Dplaying%2C%20you%20can,how%20they%20affect%20your%20communication.

How to be consistent: 6 essential tips. (2023, November 4). *Spica International.* https://www.spica.com/blog/how-to-be-consistent

How to build your personal authority. (n.d). ProjectSkills Mentor. https://projectskillsmentor.com/mentoring/how-to-build-authority

The importance of effective communication. (n.d). Stevenson University. https://www.stevenson.edu/online/about-us/news/importance-effective-communication/#:~:text=Benefits%20of%20Effective%20Communication&text=In%20situations%20where%20conflict%20does,relationship%2C%20and%20healthy%20self%20expression.

Kelly, O. (2024, May 7). *What is habit reversal training?* Verywellmind.

https://www.verywellmind.com/habit-reversal-training-2510618#toc-how-habit-reversal-training-works

Knight, R. (2014, November 5). *How to handle stress in the moment.* Harvard Business Review. https://hbr.org/2014/11/how-to-handle-stress-in-the-moment

McPheat, S. (2022, October 18). What is self-leadership and why is it important? *Management Training Specialists.* https://www.mtdtraining.com/blog/what-is-self-leadership-and-why-is-it-important.htm#:~:text=Self%2Dleadership%20is%20the%20ability,and%20reward%20yourself%20for%20success.

Miller, K. (2020, January 7). *Using self-awareness theory and skills in psychology.* PositivePsychology. https://positivepsychology.com/self-awareness-theory-skills/#:~:text=REBT%20increases%20our%20self%2Dawareness,Albert%20Ellis%20Institute%2C%20n.d.).

Morin, A. (2023, December 15). *How to face your fears when you want to tackle them head-on.* verywellmind. https://www.verywellmind.com/healthy-ways-to-face-your-fears-4165487

Negative core beliefs: what they are and how to challenge them. (n.d). *Zencare.* https://blog.zencare.co/negative-core-beliefs/

Pace, R. (2024, May 1). *How to maintain balance in a relationship: 10 practical ways*. Marriage. https://www.marriage.com/advice/relationship/maintain-balance-in-a-relationship/#10_ways_to_maintain_balance_in_a_relationship

Performance matters. (2024, February 2). HR Management. https://www.hrmanagementapp.com/performance-matters/#:~:text=High%20performers%20are%20nearly%20twice,competencies%20and%20overall%20organisational%20success.

The pillars of respect. (2021, February 12). St. Norbert College. https://www.snc.edu/respect/pillars.html

Rational emotive behavior therapy. (2024, September 25). MentalHealth. https://www.mentalhealth.com/library/rational-emotive-behavior-therapy#:~:text=REBT%20employs%20a%20range%20of,as%20unrealistic%20and%20stress%2Dinducing.

Resnick, A. (2023, July 28). *How to spot and challenge your negative core beliefs, according to a therapist*. Verywellmind. https://www.verywellmind.com/how-to-challenge-your-negative-core-beliefs-7554706

Santiago, M. (n.d). *How to find and meet your needs*. Royal Life Centers. https://royallifecenters.com/how-to-find-and-meet-your-n

eeds/#:~:text=By%20understanding%20your%20needs%2C%20you,a%20happier%2C%20more%20satisfying%20life.

Self-esteem. (2022, August). Mind. https://www.mind.org.uk/information-support/types-of-mental-health-problems/self-esteem/tips-to-improve-your-self-esteem/

Some ways to resolve conflicts. (n.d). Clackamas County. https://www.clackamas.us/ccrs/resolve.html

Your comprehensive personal needs assessment and analysis, (n.d). Personal Needs Institute. https://personalneeds.net/?language=en&tier=tier0

What is growth mindset? (n.d). Rennaisance. https://www.renaissance.com/edword/growth-mindset/#:~:text=Growth%20mindset%3A%20%E2%80%9CIn%20a%20growth,essential%20for%20great%20accomplishment.%E2%80%9D%20

www.ingramcontent.com/pod-product-compliance
Lightning Source LLC
Chambersburg PA
CBHW020534030426
42337CB00013B/842